The Musician's Handbook

A Guide to Music Fundamentals,
Hearing and Performing Music,
Reading and Writing Notation,
Improvising, and Composing

M. Carlyle Hume

Los Angeles Pierce College

Prentice Hall, Upper Saddle River, New Jersey 07458

Library of Congress Cataloging-in-Publication Data

HUME, M. CARLYLE.
   The musician's handbook : a guide to music fundamentals, hearing
and performing music, reading and writing notation, improvising, and
composing / M. Carlyle Hume.
      p.   cm.
   Includes index.
   ISBN 0-13-856709-3 (pbk. : spiral wire)
   1. Music—Theory.   2. Improvisation (Music)   3. Composition
(Music)   I. Title.
MT6.H84M87 1998
781—dc21   97-41853
                                                 CIP
                                                 MN

Editorial director: *Charlyce Jones Owen*
Publisher: *Norwell F. Therien*
Project manager: *Carole R. Crouse*
Prepress and manufacturing buyer: *Bob Anderson*
Copy editor: *Carole R. Crouse*
Marketing manager: *Sheryl Adams*

This book was set in 10.5/12 Times Roman by Stratford Publishing Services, Inc.,
and was printed and bound by Quebecor: Dubuque.
The music was set by MPT Music Engraving.
The cover was printed by Phoenix Color Corp.

PRENTICE-HALL INTERNATIONAL (UK) LIMITED, *London*
PRENTICE-HALL OF AUSTRALIA PTY. LIMITED, *Sydney*
PRENTICE-HALL CANADA INC., *Toronto*
PRENTICE-HALL HISPANOAMERICANA, S.A., *Mexico*
PRENTICE-HALL OF INDIA PRIVATE LIMITED, *New Delhi*
PRENTICE-HALL OF JAPAN, INC., *Tokyo*
SIMON & SCHUSTER ASIA PTE. LTD., *Singapore*
EDITORA PRENTICE-HALL DO BRASIL, LTDA., *Rio de Janeiro*

I dedicate this book to my loving wife, Debra,
and thank her for editing suggestions, musical advice,
and the many hours spent at the computer
transforming my manuscript into this book.

Contents

LIST OF TABLES   xi
PREFACE   xiii

chapter **1** *A Survey of Music and Its Separate Parts*   1
JUST SING IT!   1
BASIC ELEMENTS OF MUSIC: A BRIEF INTRODUCTION   1

chapter **2** *Hearing and Performing Rhythm*   6
RHYTHMIC SOUNDS AND SILENCE   6
Beat Exercise   6
Rhythm Exercises   6
METER   8
IMPROVISING SIMPLE RHYTHM COMPOSITIONS   10
ASSIGNMENT   10

chapter **3** *Hearing and Performing Pitch*   12
RANGE AND REGISTER   12
INTERVAL   12
THE TWELVE-TONE PITCH SYSTEM   13
Pitch Exercises   13
AN INTRODUCTION TO PLAYING THE PIANO   14
IMPROVISING A SIMPLE MELODY   17
ASSIGNMENT   17

chapter **4** *Rhythm Notation and Performance in Simple Meters*   19
RHYTHM NOTATION   19
PERFORMING NOTATED RHYTHMS IN $\frac{2}{4}$, $\frac{3}{4}$, AND $\frac{4}{4}$ 21
RHYTHM SYLLABLES   23
Rhythm Studies   24
REST NOTATION   25
Rhythm Studies with Rests   26
THE TIE   26
DOTTED NOTATION   27
INCOMPLETE MEASURES AND THE ANACRUSIS   27
THE FERMATA   27

DYNAMIC MARKINGS   28
    Additional Rhythm Studies   28
RHYTHM DICTATION   29
ASSIGNMENT   31
ORIGINAL RHYTHMIC COMPOSITION   33

chapter **5**   *Pitch Notation and Performance*   34

PITCH NOTATION   34
NOTATION OF THE TWELVE-TONE PITCH SYSTEM   36
PERFORMING PITCH NOTATION   36
IMPROVE YOUR NOTATION-READING SKILLS   40
MELODIC DICTATION   42
MELODY CONSTRUCTION   45
ASSIGNMENT   46
ORIGINAL MELODY NO. 1 USING PITCHES C–G   49

chapter **6**   *Scales*   50

SCALES   50
DIATONIC SCALES   50
Modal Scales   51
Equal Temperament and the Major/Minor Tonal System   52
The Major Scale   52
Minor Scales   53
    The Natural Minor Scale   53
    The Melodic Minor Scale   54
    The Harmonic Minor Scale   54
The Gypsy Scale   55
MAJOR AND MINOR PENTATONIC SCALES   55
BLUES SCALES   56
SYNTHETIC SCALES   56
The Chromatic Scale   56
    Chromaticism   57
The Whole-Tone Scale   57
The Augmented Scale   57
Diminished Scales   57
TONAL CENTER   58
TONALITY AND KEY   58
MODALITY   58
TRANSPOSING SCALES TO DIFFERENT KEYNOTES   59
ASSIGNMENT   59

chapter **7**   *Major and Minor Key Signatures*   63

KEY SIGNATURE   63
EFFECT OF ACCIDENTALS UPON THE KEY SIGNATURE   64
IDENTIFYING MAJOR AND MINOR KEYNOTES FROM KEY
    SIGNATURES   64
RELATIVE AND PARALLEL MAJOR AND MINOR SCALES   66
Musical Examples of Relative and Parallel Key Relationships   69

CONSTRUCTION OF KEY SIGNATURES   71
Writing Major and Minor Key Signatures from a Given Keynote   71
    Sequence of Sharps and Flats in Key Signatures   71
    Writing Major Key Signatures   72
    Writing Minor Key Signatures   73
The Circle of Fifths   74
HARMONIC AND MELODIC MINOR KEYS   75
IDENTIFYING THE KEY OF A COMPOSITION   77
ASSIGNMENT   79
ORIGINAL MELODY NO. 1 IN D MAJOR   82
ORIGINAL MELODY NO. 1 IN E-FLAT MAJOR   82
ORIGINAL MELODY NO. 1 IN D MINOR   83
ORIGINAL MELODY NO. 1 IN E-FLAT MINOR   83

chapter **8** *Hearing and Performing Music in Major and Minor Keys*   84

HEAR THE SCALE, HEAR THE MUSIC   84
Sight Singing   84
    Scale/Chord Drills   85
THE PRIMARY CHORDS   87
    Major Melodies   87
    Minor Melodies   89
    Melodies in Different Major and Minor Keys   91
    Melodic Dictation in Major and Minor Modes   94
ASSIGNMENT   94
ORIGINAL MELODY NO. 2 IN MAJOR   97

chapter **9** *Intervals*   98

MELODIC AND HARMONIC INTERVALS   98
IDENTIFICATION OF NOTATED INTERVALS   98
Interval Size   99
Interval Quality   99
COMPOUND INTERVALS   101
INVERTED INTERVALS   103
AURAL IDENTIFICATION OF MELODIC INTERVALS—TWO
    METHODS   104
Method One   104
Method Two   105
TWELVE BASIC INTERVAL SOUNDS   106
    Aural Melodic Interval Drills   107
IDENTIFYING HARMONIC INTERVALS
  BY SOUND—TWO METHODS   109
Method One   109
Method Two   110
    Aural Harmonic Interval Drills   112
ASSIGNMENT   113
ORIGINAL MELODY NO. 3 IN MINOR   116

chapter **10**   *Triads and Seventh Chords*   117

CHORD STRUCTURE   117
TRIAD STRUCTURE   118
IDENTIFYING TRIADS BY SOUND—TWO METHODS   119
Method One   119
Method Two   120
   Aural Triad Drills   122
TRIADS AND MAJOR SCALE RELATIONSHIPS   124
TRIADS AND MINOR SCALE RELATIONSHIPS   126
SEVENTH CHORDS IN MAJOR AND MINOR KEYS   128
Diatonic Seventh Chords in Major Keys   128
Diatonic Seventh Chords in Minor Keys   129
SCALE-DEGREE NAMES   130
THE DOMINANT SEVENTH CHORD   130
Identifying the Dominant Seventh Chord by Sound   131
TRIAD INVERSIONS   131
SEVENTH-CHORD INVERSIONS   133
USING PRIMARY CHORDS TO HARMONIZE SIMPLE
   MELODIES IN MAJOR AND MINOR KEYS   135
ASSIGNMENT   136
ORIGINAL MELODY NO. 2 IN MAJOR WITH CHORD
   ACCOMPANIMENT   138
ORIGINAL MELODY NO. 3 IN MINOR WITH CHORD
   ACCOMPANIMENT   139

chapter **11**   *More Meter and Rhythm Possibilities*   140

MULTIMETRIC COMPOSITIONS   140
$\frac{5}{4}$ METER   140
$\frac{7}{4}$ METER   141
$\frac{2}{2}$ AND ¢ METERS   142
$\frac{3}{8}$ METER   143
COMPOUND METERS   144
BORROWED RHYTHM PATTERNS   147
IRREGULAR RHYTHM PATTERNS   148
SYNCOPATED RHYTHMS   149
RHYTHMS RELATED TO THE ♫ AND ♫♫ PATTERNS   150
ASSIGNMENT   152
ORIGINAL MELODY NO. 4 IN $\frac{6}{8}$ METER
   WITH CHORD ACCOMPANIMENT   155

chapter **12**   *Chord Progressions in Major
and Minor Keys*   156

PRIMARY AND SECONDARY CHORD FUNCTIONS   156
AUTHENTIC AND PLAGAL CADENCES   156
CHORD SUBSTITUTIONS AND FREQUENTLY USED
   CHORD PROGRESSIONS   157

CHORD ROOT MOVEMENTS WITHIN HARMONIC
   PROGRESSIONS 160
Chord Progressions with Root Movements by Fifths 160
Chord Progressions with Root Movements by Seconds 161
Chord Progressions with Root Movements by Thirds 161
HARMONIZING MELODIES USING PRIMARY AND
   SECONDARY CHORDS 162
USING CHROMATIC PITCHES TO CHANGE CHORD QUALITIES 163
MODULATION 164
The Use of Common Chords and Secondary Dominant Chords
for Harmonic Modulation 164
Direct Modulation 165
ASSIGNMENT 165
ORIGINAL MELODY NO. 5 IN MAJOR WITH CHORD
   ACCOMPANIMENT 166
ORIGINAL MELODY NO. 6 IN MINOR WITH CHORD
   ACCOMPANIMENT 167

chapter **13** *Chords, Chord Symbols, and Chord Progressions
in Jazz and Popular Music* 168

CHORD SYMBOLS IN JAZZ AND POPULAR MUSIC 168
CONSTRUCTION OF CHORDS IN JAZZ AND POPULAR MUSIC 168
CHORDS AND RELATED SCALES 169
COMMON CHORD PROGRESSIONS AND
   KEYBOARD VOICINGS 169
DIATONIC AND CHROMATIC HARMONIC SUBSTITUTIONS
   AND CHORD EMBELLISHMENTS 175
CREATING HARMONIES FROM MODES 176
ASSIGNMENT 178
ORIGINAL MELODY NO. 7 WITH JAZZ-STYLE HARMONIES 178

chapter **14** *Composing a Song* 179

WHERE TO BEGIN 179
A SIX-STEP APPROACH TO SONGWRITING 180
STUDY GREAT SONGS 187
ASSIGNMENT 189
ORIGINAL SONG 189

appendix **A** *Ear-Training Exercises—Rhythm* 190

appendix **B** *Ear-Training Exercises—Pitch* 192

appendix **C** *Rhythm Studies* 196

appendix **D** *Rhythms for Dictation* 201

appendix **E** *Melodic Studies* 203

appendix **F**   *Melodies for Dictation*   209

appendix **G**   *Chord Accompaniment Patterns for Piano*   211

appendix **H**   *Recorded Examples Not Notated within Text*   213

appendix **I**   *Jazz-Style Guitar Chord Voicings*   216

appendix **J**   *Rhythms Used for Comping Jazz Harmonies*   219

Index   221

Tables

Table 1:   Rhythm Notation   19

Table 2:   Rest Notation   25

Table 3:   Intervals   102

Table 4:   The Twelve Basic Interval Sounds Related to Major Scale Degrees and Songs   108

Table 5:   The Consonant and Dissonant Characteristics of the Twelve Basic Harmonic Intervals   110

Table 6:   Consonant and Dissonant Characteristics of Triads   121

Table 7:   Diatonic Triads in Major Keys   124

Table 8:   Most Commonly Used Triads in Minor Keys   127

Table 9:   Seventh-Chord Types in Major and Minor Keys   128

Table 10:   Diatonic Seventh Chords in Major Keys   129

Table 11:   Diatonic Seventh Chords in Minor Keys   129

Table 12:   Inversion Symbols for Triads and Seventh Chords   133

Table 13:   Simple and Compound Meter Signatures   145

Table 14:   Chord Symbols and Chord Construction   170

Table 15:   Chords and Related Scales   171

Preface

Would you like to be able to perform notated music, play music "by ear," improvise, and create and notate your own music compositions? If so, *The Musician's Handbook* can help you regardless of your music background, for this text was written with the following students in mind: the beginner with no formal training, the amateur with limited skills, and the self-taught professional musician seeking more knowledge.

The Musician's Handbook presents important information about music and music performance. It is organized in a logical sequence that progresses from less-difficult to more-difficult concepts and skills. All information is presented with clearly written explanations and followed by notated and recorded examples, then reinforced through musical exercises and creative activities. The information and activities focus on the basic elements of music, ear training, performance, improvisation, and composing; the concepts and skills are applicable to all styles of music, including classical, pop, rock, folk, and jazz. Upon completion of this text, you will have an understanding of music fundamentals, the ability to read and perform notated music, and the ability to create, notate, and perform your own music compositions.

You may experience music in three ways: by listening to it; by performing someone else's compositions; and by improvising, composing, and performing your own original music. The music activities presented in *The Musician's Handbook* include experiences in all three areas. Each chapter uses the following sequence: study and memorize new information; listen to the recorded examples presented on the *compact disc* that accompanies this text; sing musical examples and play them on the piano; improvise, compose, and perform original compositions.

This textbook developed over many years and incorporates creative techniques used successfully in the classroom. Many students have been motivated to greater musical achievements by the information and creative assignments presented in this text, and you will benefit from the study of it in the same ways. You will discover the joy of performing for a live audience while receiving from your classmates and teacher the "fuel of encouragement" so important to your musical development. In addition, you will lose your fear of performance and discover that you can acquire the knowledge and develop the skills needed to express yourself through the art of music.

The most common musical experience students bring to the study of music is the *song*. Everyone has heard and performed songs from earliest childhood. For that reason, and because a simple harmonized song contains all the elements of music, *The Musician's Handbook* begins the study of music fundamentals with a song. In Chapter 1 you will be introduced to all the elements of music as they relate to a song. As you progress through the text, you will study each musical element separately in detail, but always being guided to relate the musical part to a complete musical work.

What makes this music fundamentals text unique is its creative performance approach to music study. Throughout *The Musician's Handbook* you will be asked to use your voice and the piano or an electronic keyboard instrument to execute music studies that will improve your knowledge and performance skills, which can easily be transferred to other instruments, such as the guitar, the trumpet, and the bass. If keyboard instruments are not available in the classroom or at home, sing the exercises you are studying as you move your fingers on the top of your desk as if it were a keyboard. Then arrange time to work with a keyboard instrument in one of the school practice rooms or at the home of a relative or a friend. Better yet, purchase a small, inexpensive electronic keyboard. It will be an extremely valuable tool as you pursue your study of music.

Study *The Musician's Handbook* in sequence beginning with Chapter 1, for each succeeding chapter utilizes information and performance skills presented in previous chapters. Chapters 1–10 present the information included in a college fundamentals of music class. These ten chapters will prepare you for harmony and musicianship classes that follow as part of the music major program. The remaining chapters present an introduction to materials covered in more advanced music classes, including information related to jazz/pop music theory and songwriting. As you study, continue to strengthen your performance skills and music knowledge by frequently reviewing all chapters.

Don't let the unique creative approach used in this text or the amount of information presented overwhelm you. Like the study of any new subject, the task ahead seems monumental at first. With daily effort, however, you will make continuous progress that will lead to the achievement of your goal. You will be a competent musician sooner than you may think. Remember, you *play* music, so have fun as you study the information presented in this text.

As you pursue your music studies, keep the following thought in mind. It is not "practice makes perfect." It is "*perfect* practice makes perfect." Tell yourself daily, "I can do it!" And don't forget, to succeed you must "*take action!*" Good luck!

M. Carlyle Hume

chapter 1

A Survey of Music
and Its Separate Parts

JUST SING IT!

Your study of music will begin with a single musical example that contains all the elements of music. The example is a simple song entitled *Just Sing It!* You will first survey this piece as a complete musical expression and then examine its separate parts to understand how those parts function together to form the complete composition.

Memorize the song *Just Sing It!* (recorded example 1.1). Learn to sing the vocal part the same way you would memorize a song on a new recording—play it over and over. As you listen, be aware of the overall performance, but focus on the music being sung and on the **lyrics** (words). The lyrics suggest important elements of music that you the performer *must* be aware of. Concentrate! Think of your mind as a recording machine—memorize everything you hear. See if you can sing the complete song from memory after only *three* hearings. Listen to and sing *Just Sing It!* (1.1).

Were you able to memorize this song after hearing it three times? If you were, you have exceptional tonal memory. If you memorized some of it, that's good.

BASIC ELEMENTS OF MUSIC: A BRIEF INTRODUCTION

Following is a brief introduction to the basic elements of music found in the song *Just Sing It!* A comprehensive definition and an in-depth study of each element will be presented in the following chapters.

The notation for *Just Sing It!* is provided on the next page to help you follow the song as you focus your mind and ears on its many separate elements. Don't worry if your reading skills are weak. After studying a few more chapters you *will* be reading music notation. For now, just follow the lyrics and the different symbols as they appear higher and lower on the lines.

Form in music may be thought of as a plan of construction. In the broadest sense, the form of *Just Sing It!* can be thought of as *introduction* (line 1), *main body of song* (lines 2–5), and *ending* (line 6). Follow the notation and focus on the overall form as you listen to example 1.1 again.

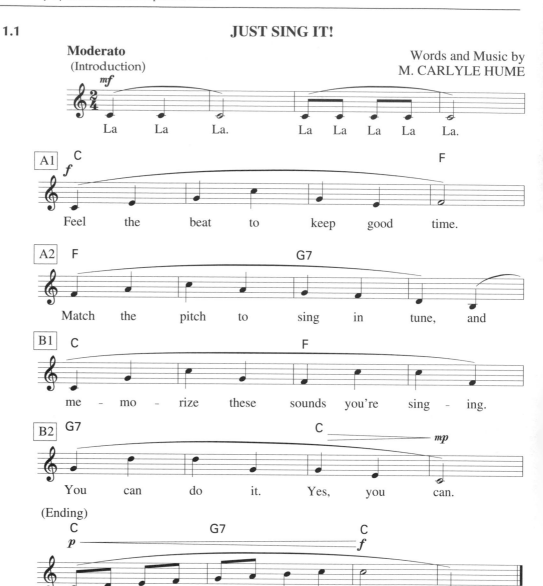

1.1   **JUST SING IT!**

Moderato
(Introduction)

Words and Music by
M. CARLYLE HUME

La   La   La.   La   La   La   La   La.

A1   C   F
Feel   the   beat   to   keep   good   time.

A2   F   G7
Match   the   pitch   to   sing   in   tune,   and

B1   C   F
me - mo - rize   these   sounds   you're   sing - ing.

B2   G7   C   *mp*
You   can   do   it.   Yes,   you   can.

(Ending)
C   G7   C
Mu - sic   can   be   fun   to   learn. Just   sing   it.

Pitch refers to the highness and lowness of sound and is related to the vibrating frequency of sound waves. The faster the vibration, the higher the pitch. As you sing the vocal part of this song with the recording, be careful to match the pitches you sing with those of the singer on the recording. You may sing this song in a higher or lower voice than the singer on the recording, but you must accurately match each pitch. If you have trouble matching pitches, practice singing the first pitch of *Just Sing It!* over and over. Slide your voice up and down like a siren until you can control your voice and match the pitch you are trying to sing. By singing this song repeatedly, you *can* learn to "sing on pitch."

NOTE: The symbol ⊙ indicates that the example is recorded on the CD that accompanies this text.

Rhythm is the durational pattern of musical sounds and silences. You hear and perform each rhythmic sound by relating its duration to the length of a recurring beat that is felt as you perform. This **beat** is the basic unit of measurement in musical time; it is like the ticking of seconds used to measure clock time in minutes and hours.

Listen again to *Just Sing It!* During the introduction the beat is heard performed on a wood block. Feel this beat and tap your toe steadily to match the **tempo** (speed of the beat). Notice that the performance of the beat stops at line A1 but the presence of the steady recurring beat continues to be *felt* throughout the entire piece. Every element of music is always performed and heard in relationship to the beat that is felt by the performer and the listener.

Listen to the introduction of example 1.1. Notice that the first two sounds (La, La) are each one beat in length, the third sound (La) is two beats in length, and the fourth, fifth, sixth, and seventh sounds (La La La La) are each a half beat in length. You must learn to perform sounds that are more than a beat long, sounds that are the same duration as the beat, and sounds that are subdivisions of the beat.

Sing example 1.1 again, and tap your toe quietly to feel the steady beat. If you feel the beat, you will keep good **time** (the complete temporal relationship of all elements as they relate to the beat). As you perform, listen for sounds that are one beat, two beats, and a half beat in duration.

A **melody** is a succession of musical tones having pitch motion (highness and lowness) and rhythmic movement. Although the length of a melody may vary, it is one of the shortest musical forms considered to be a complete aesthetic expression. The main body of the melody in example 1.1 begins at rehearsal letter A1, and it is constructed with four phrases that work together to form the complete song. A **phrase** is a natural division of the melodic line and is comparable to a complete sentence in speech. Notice how phrase A1 matches the lyrics, "Feel the beat to keep good time." The feeling of rest that comes at the end of a phrase is called a **cadence** (a resting point). Cadences can be heard both in the melody and in the **harmony** (the sound created by two or more pitches played simultaneously). Some cadences are more restful, like a period at the end of a sentence; and some cadences are less restful, like a comma that separates the elements of a compound sentence.

Listen to example 1.1 again, and notice how phrases A1 and A2 work together in a kind of question-and-answer relationship. Two phrases working together in this way form a **period**. Phrases B1 and B2 form a second period. These two periods, together with the introduction (which has two phrases) and the ending (which is one phrase), form the complete composition.

If you are still having trouble memorizing this piece, try again. This time, memorize one phrase at a time, and keep adding a phrase until you have memorized the complete composition. Phrases in music are sometimes indicated by long curved lines above the notation. Focus on phrasing and key words as suggested in example 1.2 (page 4).

The ending of *Just Sing It!* presents all the pitches that were used to create the melodic and harmonic content of this piece. This sequence of pitches is called a major scale. A **scale** is a series of pitches that are related, one to the other, both melodically and harmonically. Although music existed before scales, scales were created by musicians early in the history of music to help them organize the pitch (melodic and harmonic) elements of music. A detailed study of scales will be presented in the following chapters.

A **chord** is the simultaneous occurrence of several pitches. The **triad** is a chord consisting of three different pitches, and it is the foundation of harmony in the music of Western culture. Another chord basic to the function of harmony is the **dominant seventh chord**, a chord with four different pitches. Both the triad and the dominant

1.2   *Just Sing It!*

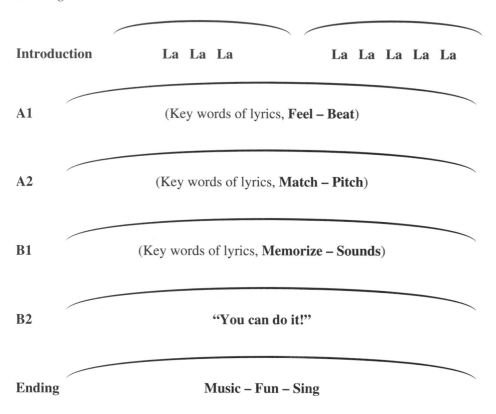

Introduction	La La La	La La La La La
A1	(Key words of lyrics, **Feel – Beat**)	
A2	(Key words of lyrics, **Match – Pitch**)	
B1	(Key words of lyrics, **Memorize – Sounds**)	
B2	**"You can do it!"**	
Ending	**Music – Fun – Sing**	

seventh chord will be studied in detail in other chapters. For now, keep in mind that chord pitches, like melody pitches, are part of the scale system.

Memorize the sound of the major scale, two different major triads, and the dominant seventh chord as you listen to and sing examples 1.3, 1.4, and 1.5. These examples are excerpts from *Just Sing It!* (page 2).

    1.3   C major scale—constructed on pitch C

Ending

Mu - sic   can   be   fun   to   learn. Just

    1.4   C major triad—constructed on 1st pitch of scale, C

F major triad—constructed on 4th pitch of scale, F

Feel the   beat

Match the   pitch

1.5   G dominant 7th chord—constructed on 5th pitch of scale, G

Sing example 1.1 again, and as you follow the notation, experience the integration of rhythm, melody, harmony, and form. Sense how the beat keeps everything tied together. Recognize the pitches of the scale as they appear in both the melody and the supporting harmony. Hear how the form gives unity to the complete composition.

There is one more element to examine and experience before more in-depth studies are pursued. **Musical expression** refers to the somewhat elusive nuances added to the composition by the performer. These nuances turn the mere combination of notes into a living, expressive art form. Expressive nuances include tempo (speed of the beat), **dynamics** (volume of notes), **phrasing** (the style of connecting or separating notes; breathing; bowing; etc.), **touch** (finger control on the keyboard or strings), and many other elements that affect the music performance. The overall character of the piece is often suggested by descriptive words—for example, Italian terms such as **dolce** (sweetly) and **passionato** (passionatcly) and English terms such as **forceful, marchlike, and joyful.** Music notation, although very accurate in setting forth rhythm and pitch, can only suggest with limited signs some of the elements of expression. Most of the elements of expression are not notated but are added at the discretion of the performer.

Examine example 1.1 again. The term **Moderato** (Italian for moderate) suggests a moderate tempo. If you sing this song at three different **tempos,** or **tempi** (plural of *tempo*)—fast (**Allegro**), moderate, and slow (**Adagio**)—you will experience three different musical expressions. This comparison will demonstrate the importance of tempo as an expressive element in music. Remember, although clock time always moves at a constant sixty seconds per minute, tempo will vary from piece to piece.

The Italian terms **forte** (loud), **piano** (soft), and **mezzo** (half) are used to notate volume. They are abbreviated as follows: *$\boldsymbol{p}$* (*piano*) indicates soft; *$\boldsymbol{mp}$* (*mezzo piano*), half or moderately soft; *$\boldsymbol{mf}$* (*mezzo forte*), moderately loud; and *$\boldsymbol{f}$* (*forte*), loud. The symbol ◁── is called a **crescendo** and indicates a gradual increase in volume. **Decrescendo** (──▷) indicates a gradual decrease in volume. All these symbols are relative, with no set value, and their interpretation is left to the performer.

Sing *Just Sing It!* again, and add the notated expressive marks to your performance. Make this performance as musical as possible.

chapter 2

Hearing and Performing Rhythm

RHYTHMIC SOUNDS AND SILENCE

Music is the art of sound, and its most basic characteristic is rhythm. Through your study and performance of the song *Just Sing It!*, you have experienced rhythmic sounds and their relationship to the beat and its tempo. Silence is also an important part of music. Like sound, silence must be measured precisely by feeling its duration in relationship to the beat. To learn the skill of keeping good musical time, you need to perform the following rhythm studies with the help of a **metronome** (a device that can be set to sound a predetermined number of pulses per minute).

Beat Exercise   Set a metronome at **M.M.** 60 (metronome marking, one beat per second) and listen to the steady ticking sound. Next, tap your toe quietly on the floor to the steady beat of the metronome (example 2.1). Keep your heel on the floor and move the toe of your shoe up and down. Notice that the beat is subdivided into two equal parts. The down (↓) movement of the foot is the first half of the beat, and the up (↑) movement of the foot is the second half of the beat.

   2.1   M.M. 60 (metronome tempo):   **Tick   Tick   Tick   Tick   Tick   Tick**   *etc.*

Steady foot tap (down-up):   ↓↑   ↓↑   ↓↑   ↓↑   ↓↑   ↓↑   *etc.*

Rhythm Exercises   Sing and play the following rhythm exercises on a piano or a synthesizer. First, study the drawing of the **keyboard** (a device with sets of twelve keys used to control the sound of the piano, synthesizer, organ, etc.); then find the G key and use it to perform each rhythmic study. As you perform, match the pitch G with your voice by singing the syllable "La." The rhythms used in exercises 2.2 through 2.9 are the same rhythms you sang while performing *Just Sing It!*

In exercise 2.2, learn to perform rhythmic sounds and silences that are one beat in duration. Sing and play one-beat sounds, which are indicated by a vertical line (|), and make no sound for a silence, which is indicated by the word "silence." Tap your foot quietly, remembering that each sound or silence will begin on the foot down (↓). As you perform this exercise repeatedly, memorize the sound of tones and silences that are one beat in duration.

2.2 M.M. 60

One tone or silence per beat, sing and play on G key: | | | **Silence** | | | **Silence**

Steady foot tap: ↓↑ ↓↑ ↓↑ ↓↑ ↓↑ ↓↑ ↓↑ ↓↑

In exercise 2.3, learn to subdivide the beat into two sounds (⊓) of equal duration. The first tone will begin on the foot down (↓), and the second tone will begin on the foot up (↑). As you perform this exercise repeatedly, memorize the sound of half-beat rhythms played on (↓) and off (↑) the beat.

2.3 M.M. 60

Two equal tones per beat, sing and play on G key: ⊓   ⊓   ⊓   **Silence**   ⊓   ⊓   ⊓   **Silence**

Steady foot tap: ↓↑ ↓↑ ↓↑ ↓↑ ↓↑ ↓↑ ↓↑ ↓↑

In exercise 2.4, learn to perform sounds for two full beats (⊔). The tone will begin on the foot down (↓) and continue through the foot up (↑) of the first beat and the down (↓) and up (↑) of the second beat.

2.4 M.M. 60

One tone held for two beats, sing and play on G key: ⌴   ⌴   ⌴   ⌴

Steady foot tap: ↓↑ ↓↑ ↓↑ ↓↑ ↓↑ ↓↑ ↓↑ ↓↑

Learn to perform rhythmic patterns that combine one-beat, two-beat, and half-beat tones and one-beat silences. Follow the graphic symbols in exercises 2.5 through 2.9, and as you perform, feel and hear each rhythm in relationship to the down (↓)–up (↑) subdivision of each beat.

2.5 M.M. 60

Sing and play on G key: | | ⌴ | | ⌴

Steady foot tap: ↓↑ ↓↑ ↓↑ ↓↑ ↓↑ ↓↑ ↓↑ ↓↑

2.6 M.M. 60

Sing and play on G key: | | ⊓ | ⊓ | | **Silence**

Steady foot tap: ↓↑ ↓↑ ↓↑ ↓↑ ↓↑ ↓↑ ↓↑ ↓↑

2.7   M.M. 60

Sing and play on G key:

Steady foot tap:

2.8   M.M. 60

Sing and play on G key: **Silence**

Steady foot tap:

2.9   M.M. 60

Sing and play on G key:

Steady foot tap:

METER

In most music the recurring beat is grouped into **accented** (strong) and **unaccented** (weak) beats that establish the **meter.** There are only two basic meter groupings: duple meter and triple meter. In **duple meter** the beat is grouped in twos: strong (**1**), weak (2). Listen to and perform example 2.10; play and sing beat numbers using the pitch G.

2.10   Duple meter

1 2, **1** 2, **1** 2, **1** 2

Exercises 2.2 through 2.6 are in duple meter. Perform them again as you feel duple-meter beats (strong, weak).

In **triple meter** the beat is grouped in threes: strong (**1**), weak (2), weak (3). Listen to and perform example 2.11; play and sing beat numbers using the pitch G.

2.11   Triple meter

1 2 3, **1** 2 3, **1** 2 3, **1** 2 3

Exercises 2.7 through 2.9 are in triple meter. Perform them again as you feel triple-meter beats (strong, weak, weak).

All other meter groupings are combinations of duple and triple meters. For example, four is 2 + 2; five is 2 + 3 or 3 + 2; six is 3 + 3 or 2 + 2 + 2; seven is 2 + 3 + 2 or 3 + 2 + 2 or 2 + 2 + 3. Because quadruple meter is so widely used, it will be introduced here along with duple meter and triple meter; other meters will be studied later in the book.

In **quadruple meter** the beat is grouped in fours. Because quadruple meter is really a duple-meter feel (2 + 2), it has two accented beats in each meter grouping: strongest (primary accent **1**); weak (2); moderately strong (secondary accent 3); weak (4). It could be argued that the beats 1 and 3 are felt with the same accent, and that quadruple meter is used instead of duple meter only for convenience of notation. Listen to and perform example 2.12; play and sing beat numbers using the pitch G.

2.12   Quadruple meter

1 2 3 4, **1** 2 3 4, **1** 2 3 4, **1** 2 3 4

Exercises 2.2 through 2.6 can also be performed feeling quadruple-meter beats.

2.13   Learn to perform exercises 2.2 through 2.9 playing the rhythm part with the right hand on the G key while playing the basic beat with the left hand on the C key. Also learn to perform these exercises at tempos faster and slower than M.M. 60.

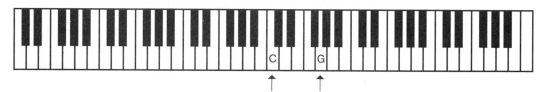

Left-hand basic beat   Right-hand rhythm part

There are only two basic meter groupings: duple and triple. There are, however, four basic meters: simple duple, simple triple, compound duple, and compound triple. With *Just Sing It!* and all the exercises in this chapter, you have been experiencing **simple duple meter** and **simple triple meter,** in which the music subdivides the beat into twos and multiples of two. **Compound duple meter** and **compound triple meter,** in which the music subdivides the beat into threes and multiples of three, will be studied in Chapter 11.

Your awareness of meter and the complex interaction of meter with other rhythmic, melodic, and harmonic elements will increase as your in-depth study of music continues. As you listen to music, be aware that the meter beats are *silent*; and because the meter beats are silent, the meter-beat accents are also silent. It is you, the performer or listener, who must *feel* the meter beats and their accents as they interact with all the elements of the music.

The song *Just Sing It!* (example 1.1) is in duple meter. Listen to it again as you feel duple-meter beats (strong, weak). Next, sing this song as you feel it in duple meter. Finally, try singing *Just Sing It!* as a triple-meter song (strong, weak, weak) by holding the first note of each meter grouping one additional beat.

Duple, triple, and quadruple meters are used extensively in all forms and styles of music. Now that you have established an awareness of these meters, listen to a variety of recorded music examples and clap the meter beats that you think should accompany the music you are hearing. Remember to feel an accent on the first beat of each meter grouping, and in quadruple meter to place a lesser accent on the third beat of each meter grouping. Following are some suggested titles for listening.

SIMPLE DUPLE METER

Stars and Stripes Forever, by John P. Sousa

Yankee Doodle, Traditional

SIMPLE TRIPLE METER

Symphony in B minor (*Unfinished*), by Franz Schubert

The Star-Spangled Banner, by Francis S. Key and John S. Smith

SIMPLE QUADRUPLE METER

Hallelujah Chorus from *Messiah,* by George F. Handel

When the Saints Go Marchin' In, Spiritual

IMPROVISING SIMPLE RHYTHM COMPOSITIONS

Improvisation is a form of spontaneous music creation, composing as you perform. To prepare for rhythmic improvisation experiences, listen to and learn to perform example 2.14. This simple rhythm composition will serve as a model for your improvisations. It is in triple meter and is performed at a moderate tempo, and the rhythms used are either one beat, two beats, or a half beat in length. One-beat silences are also used. These are the rhythmic elements you learned to perform in exercises 2.2 through 2.9. On the recording the basic beat is performed with the left hand on the C key, and the rhythm part is played with the right hand on the G key above the left-hand C key. Memorize this piece without consulting the notation on the following page; then learn to play it "by ear" on the piano.

Learn to improvise rhythm pieces by using the following procedure.

1. Use the piano to perform your rhythmic improvisations.

2. Choose a tempo and a meter for each of your improvisations. The tempo may be slow, moderate, or fast. The meter may be duple (strong, weak) or triple (strong, weak, weak).

3. Start a metronome ticking and begin playing meter beats on the C key with your left hand as you tap steady beats with your foot. Listen to the beat until you feel that you have firmly established the meter and the tempo. When you *feel* the steady beat, begin improvising superimposed rhythms in time with the beat. Use your right hand to play the improvised rhythms on the G key above the C key. Do not try to think of a rhythmic idea before you begin. Play the first tone, and you will instinctively know whether the next rhythm is to be long or short, on the beat or off the beat. Use one-beat, two-beat, and half-beat sounds and one-beat silences. Remember, there is no right or wrong rhythm piece. Just feel the steady meter beats and perform spontaneous rhythm patterns.

   If you experience trouble playing the beat with the left hand as you improvise with the right hand, learn to improvise rhythms with only the right hand playing in time with the steady tap of your foot. When you become proficient at this, add the left hand playing the meter beats on the piano.

4. The rhythm patterns you create should work together to make a musical statement, and the beat is the glue that holds your piece together. To help structure your improvisations, repeat some of the short rhythmic ideas you create; other ideas should be followed by new ideas that contrast with the previous rhythms. Your pieces should be twenty to thirty seconds in length. In any case, continue improvising until you feel your piece is finished.

ASSIGNMENT

1. Practice improvising many rhythm pieces using the piano. Use different tempos, meters, and rhythms, and make your pieces as musically expressive as possible by adding dynamics to your improvisations.

2. Create and prepare for a performance a triple-meter rhythm piece that lasts no longer than thirty seconds. Memorize your original piece and play it on the piano for your class, friends, or family. Use example 2.14 as a model.

2.14   **Moderato**

chapter 3

Hearing and Performing Pitch

RANGE AND REGISTER

You have experienced the highness and lowness of pitch by singing the song *Just Sing It!* Now experience a wider **pitch range** (the full extent of highness and lowness) by playing different keys up and down the piano keyboard (see the following illustration). The division of pitch into groups of similar low, middle, and high pitch qualities is called **register.** Although the human voice is more limited in its range than, for example, the trumpet, and the trumpet more limited in its range than the piano, all voices and instruments have their own low, middle, and high registers.

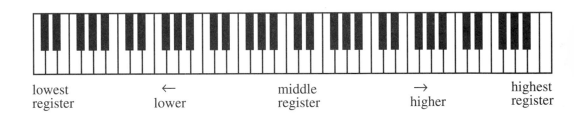

| lowest register | ← lower | middle register | → higher | highest register |

INTERVAL

An **interval** is the distance between two pitches, and the smallest interval in Western music is a **half step.** Experience the sound of a half-step interval. See the following illustration.

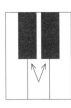

Half step: To produce the sound of a half-step interval, play back and forth from a white key to the nearest black key below or above.

THE TWELVE-TONE PITCH SYSTEM

The music of Western culture uses only twelve pitches. These pitches are the tones of the **twelve-tone pitch system**; they are a half step apart and can be produced by playing the seven white keys and five black keys of the piano. The **white keys** produce **natural** (♮) pitches identified by the first seven letters of the alphabet: **A, B, C, D, E, F, G.** Each successive letter represents a higher pitch: B is higher than A, C is higher than B, and so on. The **black keys** produce **sharp** (♯) pitches, natural pitches raised a half step, and **flat** (♭) pitches, natural pitches lowered a half step. These pitch alteration signs (naturals ♮, sharps ♯, flats ♭) are called **accidentals.** Because the twelve tones of this pitch system can be reproduced in different registers from low to high, a wide range of tones are available. Study and play on the piano the pitches of the twelve-tone pitch system. See the illustration below.

The distance from one pitch to a second pitch eight letters above or below it is called an **octave** (**C,** D, E, F, G, A, B **C; E-flat,** F, G, A, B, C, D, **E-flat**). Each octave contains the same twelve pitches, but each set of pitches sounds at a higher or lower register. Study and play different twelve-tone pitch sets within different octaves (e.g., A to A, C to C, E to E). See the illustration below.

As you play and study the pitches related to the keyboard, notice that each black key produces one tone but represents both a sharp and a flat pitch (e.g., A♯ and B♭). Pitches that are identified by two different names but sound the same are called **enharmonic pitches.** Their use will be explained later in the book.

Look again at the keyboard and notice that there are no black keys between white keys B and C and white keys E and F. That is because these natural pitches are a half step apart. *Memorize* that the pitches B to C and E to F are a half step apart; all other natural pitches (A–B, C–D, D–E, F–G, and G–A) are a **whole step** (two half steps) apart. Play half-step and whole-step sounds between different pitches represented on the keyboard (see the following illustration), and *memorize* the slight difference in sound between the two intervals (e.g., half step B–C, whole step B–C♯; half step D–E♭, whole step D–E; etc.).

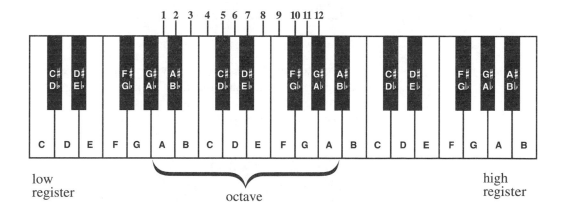

Pitch Exercises   Play various pitches on the piano. Learn to sing them by moving the sound of your voice up or down until your voice matches exactly the pitch being produced on the piano. You will hear and even feel a pure, clear, smooth sound when you match tones. When you match pitches well, you are "singing in tune." Sometimes the pitch you want to match will be too high or too low for your voice to reach. Simply sing the same pitch down or up an octave, in the register below or above the tone you want to match. If you are singing in tune, you will produce the same clear, smooth sound.

Choose pitches in different registers of the keyboard to match with your voice.

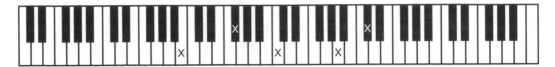

AN INTRODUCTION TO PLAYING THE PIANO

Begin your study by becoming more familiar with the piano keyboard. Notice that the keyboard has both white and black keys and that the black keys are arranged in alternating groups of two keys and three keys. The first white key to the left of each group of two black keys is the pitch C, and the C nearest the center of the keyboard is "middle" C (see illustration A).

A

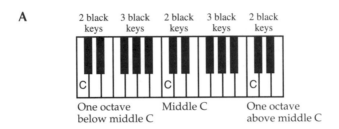

When you have found the pitch C on the keyboard, you can find D by moving one white key to the right of C, E by moving one white key to the right of D. The pitches F and G are the following white keys to the right (see illustration B).

B

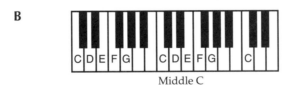

Melodies or chords may be played on the piano with either the right or the left hand. For convenience, the fingers of each hand are numbered 1 through 5 from the thumb to the little finger, and the finger numbers are associated with different pitches on the keyboard (see illustration C).

C

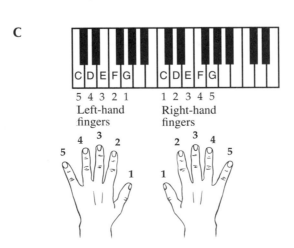

Place the thumb (1) of the right hand on middle C; then curve the remaining fingers so they rest comfortably on the keys D (2nd finger), E (3rd), F (4th), and G (5th). Practice playing up and down these pitches (C, D, E, F, G) over and over. Play to a steady beat and repeat until you become skilled at striking and releasing one pitch after the other. Then place the little finger (5) of the left hand on the C key an octave below middle C. With your left hand, practice the same drill that you just played with your right hand.

After you have gained some skill with the preceding exercises, learn to hear and perform exercises 3.1 through 3.9. These exercises use the first five pitches of the C major scale (C, D, E, F, G), the C major triad (C, E, G), and three of the four pitches of the G dominant seventh chord (G, F, D). You will recognize these familiar pitch patterns from your experience performing *Just Sing It!* (examples 1.3–1.5). Use the following procedure.

1. Play each exercise on the piano, first with the right hand, then with the left hand, and finally with both hands simultaneously. As you play, memorize the following: the sound of each pitch, its relationship to the scale, its relationship to the chord, the duration of its sound, and its relationship to the beat. Memorize these sounds as you would a recorded song you wanted to sing. Perform the exercises with the metronome ticking and your foot tapping a steady beat (M.M. 60).

2. Sing each exercise as you play it on the piano. Practice until you can sing it in time (with the beat) and in tune.

3. Give yourself only the sound of the first pitch from the piano. Then sing each exercise without playing the piano.

3.1 C major scale pattern

M.M. 60, duple meter

Play and sing (pitch letters), one pitch per beat:	C	D	E	F	G	F	E	D
Right-hand fingering:	1	2	3	4	5	4	3	2
Left-hand fingering:	5	4	3	2	1	2	3	4

Steady foot tap:

3.2 C major scale pattern

M.M. 60, duple meter

Play and sing (pitch letters), two equal pitches per beat:	C D	E F	G F	E D	C D	E F	G F	E D
Right-hand fingering:	1 2	3 4	5 4	3 2	1 2	3 4	5 4	3 2
Left-hand fingering:	5 4	3 2	1 2	3 4	5 4	3 2	1 2	3 4

Steady foot tap:

3.3 C major triad

M.M. 60, triple meter

Play and sing:	C	E	G	G	E	C	C	G E	C
Right-hand fingering:	1	3	5	5	3	1	1	5 3	1
Left-hand fingering:	5	3	1	1	3	5	5	1 3	5

Steady foot tap:

3.4　C major triad

M.M. 60, duple meter

Play and sing:	C C	E E	G G	Silence	G G	E E	C C	Silence
Right-hand fingering:	1 1	3 3	5 5		5 5	3 3	1 1	
Left-hand fingering:	5 5	3 3	1 1		1 1	3 3	5 5	

Steady foot tap:

3.5　C major triad

M.M. 60, triple meter

Play and sing:	C	G	C	C C	G G	C	C E	G E	C
Right-hand fingering:	1	5	1	1 1	5 5	1	1 3	5 3	1
Left-hand fingering:	5	1	5	5 5	1 1	5	5 3	1 3	5

Steady foot tap:

3.6　C major scale pattern and triad

M.M. 60, duple meter

Play and sing:	C D	E F	G F	E D	C E	G E	C G	C
Right-hand fingering:	1 2	3 4	5 4	3 2	1 3	5 3	1 5	1
Left-hand fingering:	5 4	3 2	1 2	3 4	5 3	1 3	5 1	5

Steady foot tap:

3.7　G dominant seventh chord

M.M. 60, triple meter

Play and sing:	G	F	D	G	F	D	C	G E	C
Right-hand fingering:	5	4	2	5	4	2	1	5 3	1
Left-hand fingering:	1	2	4	1	2	4	5	1 3	5

Steady foot tap:

3.8　G dominant seventh chord

M.M. 60, duple meter

Play and sing:	G G	F F	G G	D D	D F	G F	D G	C
Right-hand fingering:	5 5	4 4	5 5	2 2	2 4	5 4	2 5	1
Left-hand fingering:	1 1	2 2	1 1	4 4	4 2	1 2	4 1	5

Steady foot tap:

3.9   Perform exercises 3.1–3.8 at faster and slower tempos.

IMPROVISING A SIMPLE MELODY

Improvised melodies, like improvised rhythm pieces, are created spontaneously. To prepare for melodic improvisation experiences, listen to and learn to perform example 3.10. This simple melody, like *Just Sing It!*, will help to develop your performance skills and increase your knowledge of music elements such as pitch, rhythm, melodic phrasing, and form. It is in duple meter and is performed at a moderate tempo. Its form consists of four phrases (two periods), and it uses the first five pitches of the C major scale. The melodic movement is by scale tones (C, D, E, F, G) and by C major (C, E, G) and G dominant seventh (G, F, D) chord tones. The rhythms are one beat, two beats, or a half beat in length.

As you listen, notice that this melody uses the same musical elements you learned to perform in exercises 3.1 through 3.8. Notice, too, that each phrase uses repeated rhythmic and melodic ideas to strengthen the melody's form. *Memorize* this piece, and learn to sing it and to play it on the piano. Do this by ear, without consulting the notation on the following page.

Learn to improvise melodies by using the following procedure.

1. Use the piano and your voice to perform your improvised melodies.
2. Think of a mood or a style you would like to express with each of your improvised melodies. Then choose a tempo and a meter that will help express the mood or the style you have in mind.
3. Start a metronome ticking and begin tapping meter beats with your foot. Listen to the beat until you feel that you have firmly established the meter and the tempo. Then, in time, begin improvising a melody that uses pitches C, D, E, F, and G. Do not try to think of an appropriate melodic idea before you begin. Simply play C, E, or G for the first note of your melody. Then you will instinctively know how quickly to move to the next pitch and whether that pitch should be higher or lower or if your melody should move by scale or chord tones. Remember that there is no right or wrong melodic or rhythmic sequence. Just listen to the beat and play spontaneous melodic ideas. End your melody on the pitch C.
4. The melodic patterns you create should work together to make a musical statement, and the beat is the glue that holds your piece together. Structure each of your improvised melodies by forming phrases and periods with repeated and contrasting melodic and rhythmic ideas. Review the information in Chapter 1 (page 3) regarding phrases, periods, and cadences. Think of your melodic ideas as a musical dialogue: melodic question, melodic answer, melodic question, melodic answer, and so on. *Play only what you hear. Don't just move your fingers up and down the keyboard.* Your melodies may be as short as twenty seconds in length. In any case, continue improvising each melody until you feel it is finished.

ASSIGNMENT

1. Practice improvising many melodies on the piano. Use different meters, tempos, and rhythms, and the pitches C, D, E, F, and G. Add dynamics to your improvised pieces; always strive to make your melodies as musically expressive as possible.
2. Create and prepare for a performance a duple-meter melody using the pitches C, D, E, F, and G. Your piece should last no longer than thirty seconds, and it should be constructed with four phrases and have varied dynamics. Memorize your orig-

inal melody and play it on the piano for your class, friends, or family. Use example 3.10 as a model.

chapter 4

Rhythm Notation and Performance in Simple Meters

RHYTHM NOTATION

Rhythm is written with symbols that represent the duration of musical sounds and silences. Both the writing process and the symbols are called **notation.**

Table 1 shows the basic rhythm symbols used to notate traditional music sounds. These symbols are called **notes.** The duration of each note is referred to as its **note value.** There is, however, no absolute durational value for notes. Each note's duration, as explained later, will vary depending upon the meter and the tempo of the piece. As

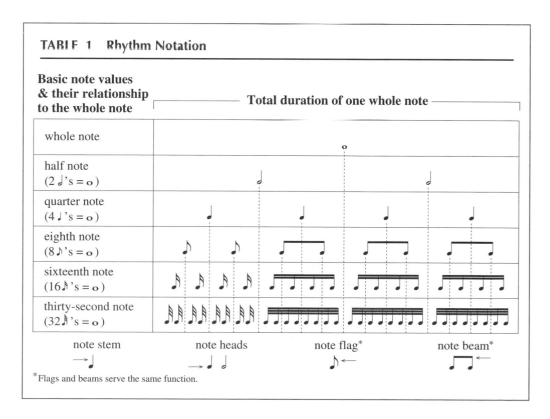

TABLE 1   Rhythm Notation

*Flags and beams serve the same function.

you study Table 1, notice the 2:1 ratio that exists between the notes (e.g., 2 quarter notes = 1 half note). This 2:1 ratio between notes remains constant regardless of the meter or the tempo.

Study the following example and the explanation that follows.

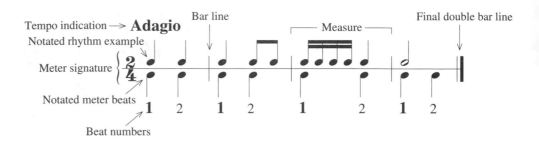

Rhythms are notated in groups according to the meter of the piece. Vertical lines, called **bar lines,** are used to separate these meter groupings so that the notation will be easy to read. The space between two bar lines, called a **measure,** contains one complete meter grouping. A **double bar line** (‖) indicates the end of a complete section of music. A **final double bar line** (‖) indicates the end of a piece. Beat 1, the strongest meter beat, is always placed immediately following the bar line.

The meter of a composition is indicated at the beginning of the music notation by two numbers, one placed above the other. These numerals, the **meter signature** or **time signature** (the terms are synonymous), indicate the meter and designate which note will represent one beat. **Simple meters** use **simple notes** (notes without a dot ♩ ♪ ♫, etc.) to represent the meter beat, and each beat and its representative note can be subdivided into two equal parts and the parts further divided into four parts, eight parts, and so on. **Compound meters,** discussed in Chapter 11, use **compound notes** (notes with a dot ♩. ♪. ♫., etc.) to represent the meter beat. In simple meters the top numeral indicates the meter, the number of beats per measure; the bottom numeral indicates which note represents one beat. Following are the interpretations of some common simple meter signatures. Additional simple meters are presented in Chapter 11.

SIMPLE DUPLE METER

$\frac{2}{4}$ is called "two four meter" or two four time."

    2 = duple meter, two beats per measure

    4 = quarter note receives one beat

SIMPLE TRIPLE METER

$\frac{3}{4}$ is called "three four meter" or "three four time."

    3 = triple meter, three beats per measure

    4 = quarter note receives one beat

SIMPLE QUADRUPLE METER

$\frac{4}{4}$ is called "four four meter" or "four four time."

    4 = quadruple meter, four beats per measure

    4 = quarter note receives one beat

Because of its extensive use, $\frac{4}{4}$ meter is sometimes called **common time;** the common time meter signature, **C**, may be used in place of the $\frac{4}{4}$ meter signature.

C = quadruple meter, four beats per measure and quarter note receives one beat

The tempo of a composition may be indicated by descriptive terms in Italian, German, French, or English. These terms are placed at the beginning of the piece above the first measure. Italian terms are most widely used, and the most common terms are **adagio** (slow), **moderato** (moderate), and **allegro** (fast). Some composers prefer to be more accurate in their tempo indications and choose to use metronome markings (e.g., M.M. 120) in place of general terms.

PERFORMING NOTATED RHYTHMS IN $\frac{2}{4}$, $\frac{3}{4}$, AND $\frac{4}{4}$

To begin performing simple rhythm pieces notated in $\frac{2}{4}$, $\frac{3}{4}$, and $\frac{4}{4}$ meters, you need to understand note values in these meters and how they relate to the beat and the tempo. Because all rhythms are measured by their relationship to the beat, it is necessary that you feel the recurring pulse of the beat at all times while you are performing. Using a metronome and tapping the beat *quietly* with your foot will help you do this.

Study the following note values as they apply to $\frac{2}{4}$, $\frac{3}{4}$, and $\frac{4}{4}$ meters. Then study and perform each exercise; play it on the piano using the pitch G as you sing "la" on the same pitch.

A **quarter note** $\downarrow$ receives one beat—sustain from one foot tap to the next.

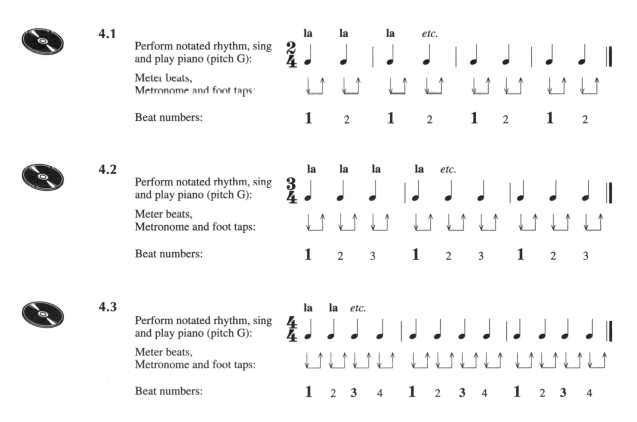

Two **eighth notes** ♪♪ together receive one beat—one half of a beat each, one when the foot is down and one when the foot is up.

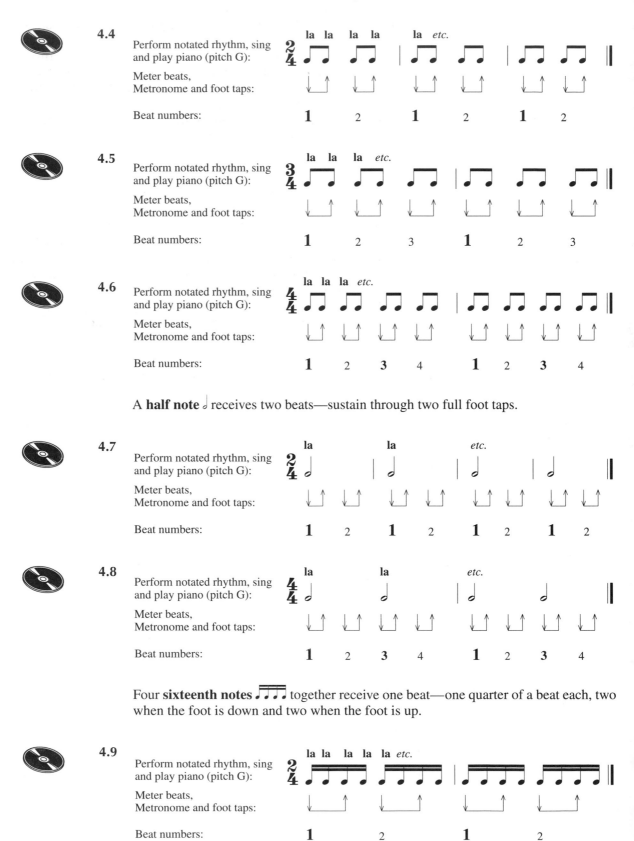

A **half note** ♩ receives two beats—sustain through two full foot taps.

Four **sixteenth notes** ♬♬ together receive one beat—one quarter of a beat each, two when the foot is down and two when the foot is up.

4.10

Perform notated rhythm, sing
and play piano (pitch G):

Meter beats,
Metronome and foot taps:

Beat numbers:

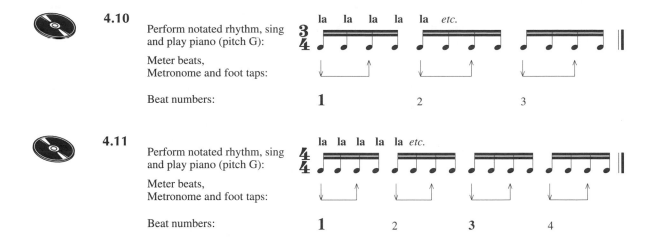

4.11

Perform notated rhythm, sing
and play piano (pitch G):

Meter beats,
Metronome and foot taps:

Beat numbers:

RHYTHM SYLLABLES

Many people find it helpful to recite rhythm syllables when learning to perform
rhythms. Study the following rhythm syllable system.

For notes that fall on the beat (foot down), recite the beat number upon which the
note falls.

Rhythm syllables:

Notated rhythm:

Part of beat note falls on:

Foot tap:

Beat numbers:

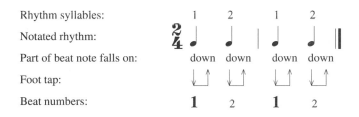

For a note that falls on the second half of the beat (foot up), recite the syllable
"an."

Rhythm syllables:

Notated rhythm:

Part of beat note falls on:

Foot tap:

Beat numbers:

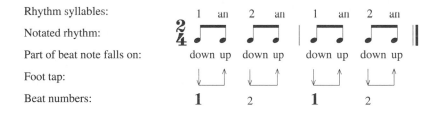

For a note that falls on the second and fourth quarters of the beat, recite the syllable "ee" for the second quarter of the beat and "da" for the fourth quarter of the beat.

Rhythm syllables:

Notated rhythm:

Part of beat note falls on:

Foot tap:

Beat numbers:

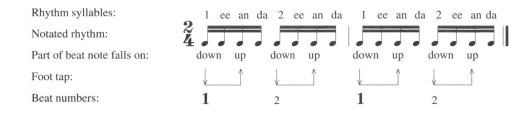

For notes with values of more than one beat, recite two or more syllables, making an effort to blend all syllables into one continuous sound for the full length of the note.

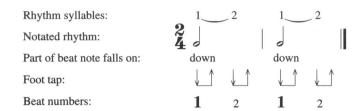

Keep in mind that tapping your foot and thinking down-up, or reciting rhythm syllables, is only a learning aid to help you hear rhythms that are notated. Your goal in rhythm performance is to hear the sound of the notated rhythm in your mind as you read. Musicians do not think down-up or rhythm syllables when performing; they simply hear the sound of the notated symbols in relationship to the beat they are feeling. Perform exercises 4.1 through 4.11 again, this time singing rhythm syllables. If you find the syllables helpful, use them to perform other exercises in this chapter.

Rhythm Studies   Examine and perform the following rhythm studies. Tap your foot to feel the beat as you sing and play the rhythm notated above the horizontal line. Use the pitch G, and sing rhythm syllables or the word "la."

After you become proficient at singing and playing the rhythm part above the line, perform both the rhythm part and the meter beats on the piano. Play the rhythm part above the line with your right hand on the pitch G, and the beat notated below the line with your left hand on the pitch C below G.

 4.12

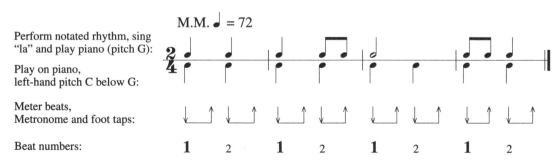

 4.13

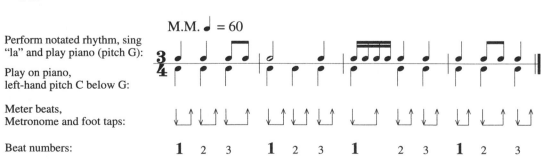

4.14

Perform notated rhythm, sing
"la" and play piano (pitch G):

Play on piano,
left-hand pitch C below G:

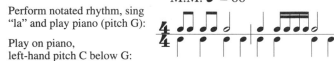

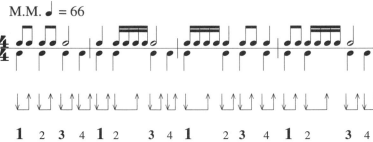

Meter beats,
Metronome and foot taps:

Beat numbers:

1 2 3 4 1 2   3 4 1   2 3 4 1 2   3 4

4.15

Perform notated rhythm, sing
"la" and play piano (pitch G):

Play on piano,
left-hand pitch C below G:

Meter beats,
Metronome and foot taps:

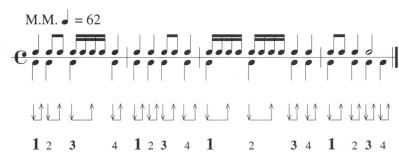

Beat numbers:

1 2 3   4 1 2 3 4 1   2   3 4 1 2 3 4

REST NOTATION

A silence in music is called a **rest.** Like rhythmic sounds, rests have notation symbols
that indicate time value. These rest symbols, like notes, have no absolute value; their
value depends upon the meter and the tempo. Nevertheless, the 2:1 ratio between
rests remains constant regardless of the meter or the tempo. In $\frac{2}{4}$, $\frac{3}{4}$, and $\frac{4}{4}$ meters the
quarter rest (𝄽) receives one beat, the **half rest** (–) receives two beats, the **eighth rest**
(𝄾) receives one half beat, and so on. Although there will be no singing or playing of an
instrument when you perform a rest (silence), the beat continues to recur steadily, so
you will have a means to measure the length of the silence. Study Table 2.

TABLE 2 Rest Notation																
Basic rest values & their relationship to the whole rest	**Total duration of one whole rest**															
whole rest								–								
half rest (2 – 's = –)				–								–				
quarter rest (4 𝄽 's = –)		𝄽				𝄽				𝄽				𝄽		
eighth rest (8 𝄾 's = –)	𝄾		𝄾		𝄾		𝄾		𝄾		𝄾		𝄾		𝄾	
sixteenth rest (16 𝄿 's = –)	𝄿	𝄿	𝄿	𝄿	𝄿	𝄿	𝄿	𝄿	𝄿	𝄿	𝄿	𝄿	𝄿	𝄿	𝄿	𝄿
thirty-second rest (32 𝄿 's = –)	𝄿𝄿	𝄿𝄿	𝄿𝄿	𝄿𝄿	𝄿𝄿	𝄿𝄿	𝄿𝄿	𝄿𝄿	𝄿𝄿	𝄿𝄿	𝄿𝄿	𝄿𝄿	𝄿𝄿	𝄿𝄿	𝄿𝄿	𝄿𝄿

Rhythm Studies with Rests   Practice performing the following exercises (4.16–4.20). Sing "la" or rhythm syllables as you play the piano. Continue using a metronome, and perform these exercises at different tempos, from slow (M.M. 60) to fast (M.M. 120). For additional rhythm exercises, see Appendix C, Rhythm Studies.

4.16

Sing and play on piano, right-hand pitch G:

Play on piano, left-hand pitch C below G:

4.17

Sing and play on piano, right-hand pitch G:

Play on piano, left-hand pitch C below G:

4.18

Sing and play on piano, right-hand pitch G:

Play on piano, left-hand pitch C below G:

4.19

Sing and play on piano, right-hand pitch G:

Play on piano, left-hand pitch C below G:

4.20

Sing and play on piano, right-hand pitch G:

Play on piano, left-hand pitch C below G:

THE TIE

A **tie** ♩‿♩ is a curved line connecting two adjacent notes of the same pitch and indicates that the two notes are to be performed as one continuous sound held for the combined duration of the notes. Ties connect note heads and may be written across bar lines or within measures. Study, listen to, and perform the following recorded example.

4.21   Moderato

DOTTED NOTATION

A dot may be used in conjunction with notes (♩. ♪.) for notation convenience and ease of reading. For example, the rhythm ♩ ♩ can be more easily written and read when notated as ♩.—both the tie and the quarter note are eliminated by using the dot. The **dot** always adds to the duration of the preceding note one-half of that note's value. For example, in $\frac{4}{4}$ meter, a half note (♩) equals 2 beats and a **dotted half note** (♩. 2+1) equals 3 beats; a quarter note (♩) equals 1 beat and a **dotted quarter note** (♩. 1+½) equals 1½ beats. Notes with dots are also called **compound notes.** Compare, listen to, and perform the following identical rhythms; example 4.22a uses tied notes and example 4.22b uses dotted notes.

4.22a   **Moderato**

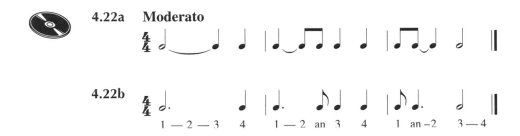

4.22b

INCOMPLETE MEASURES AND THE ANACRUSIS

Often you will come across pieces that begin with an **incomplete measure**—that is, a measure containing fewer beats than indicated by the time signature. In these cases, the note or notes that make up the incomplete measure are referred to as an **anacrusis** or a **pickup.** When performed, the anacrusis gives the feeling of leading into the primary accent (beat 1) of the first full measure. The beats missing from the incomplete measure must be accounted for and are always found in the last measure of the piece or in the last measure of a section of music in an extended work made up of several sections. Listen to, study, and perform the following recorded examples.

4.23   **Moderato**

4.24   **Moderato**

THE FERMATA

The **fermata** (𝄐), also referred to as a **hold,** indicates that the note or the rest over which the fermata appears should be held for approximately twice its value. This is a general rule, however, and at the choice of the conductor or the performer the fermata may be held for a longer or shorter duration. While the fermata is being held, the beat stops; therefore, the note or the rest is not heard in relationship to the pulse of the meter. The meter and the tempo are resumed immediately following the fermata, unless it is placed, as it is in most cases, above the last note of the piece. The fermata should be used only as a dramatic effect to stop the momentum of the piece. Study, listen to, and perform the following recorded example.

4.25   Moderato

DYNAMIC MARKINGS

The expressive quality of the rhythm pieces you perform may be enhanced by the use of changing volume levels. Study the following **dynamic markings** used in music notation to indicate changes in volume. These symbols are placed below notated instrumental music and above vocal music when lyrics appear below the staff. The volume each symbol represents continues from measure to measure until another dynamic change is introduced.

> For a loud volume use the letter *f*, the Italian abbreviation for **forte** (loud).
>
> For a very loud volume use the letters *ff*, the Italian abbreviation for **fortissimo** (very loud).
>
> For a soft volume use the letter *p*, the Italian abbreviation for **piano** (soft).
>
> For a very soft volume use the letters *pp*, the Italian abbreviation for **pianissimo** (very soft).
>
> The letter *m*, the Italian abbreviation for **mezzo** (moderate), may be used with *forte* and *piano*: *mf*, moderately loud; *mp*, moderately soft.
>
> Use a **crescendo** sign ⎯◁ to indicate a gradual increase in volume.
>
> Use a **decrescendo** or **diminuendo** sign ▷⎯ to indicate a gradual decrease in volume.

Additional Rhythm Studies   Study and perform the following rhythm studies (4.26–4.33). As you perform, keep in mind that each dynamic marking indicates the volume that applies to the rhythms written above and below the line and that the volume continues from measure to measure until another dynamic appears. Continue practicing with a metronome.

4.26

Sing and play on piano, right-hand pitch G:

Play on piano, left-hand pitch C below G:

Allegro

4.27

Sing and play on piano, right-hand pitch G:

Play on piano, left-hand pitch C below G:

Adagio

4.28 Moderato

4.29 Allegro

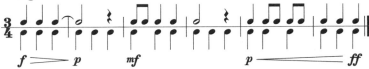

4.30 Moderato

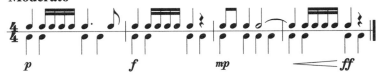

4.31 Adagio

4.32 Adagio

4.33 Adagio

RHYTHM DICTATION

Because music is an aural art, you must develop your listening perception to the highest possible level. You must learn to memorize the rhythmic sounds you hear and then translate them into notation. Notating rhythms you hear is called **rhythm dictation.**
Use the following procedure to notate dictated rhythms.

1. Tap your foot quietly so that you can feel the beat, the meter, and the tempo of the music being performed on the recording or by the person playing the dictated rhythm.

2. Listen to the dictated rhythmic pattern and memorize it.

3. Hear in your mind the rhythmic pattern you have memorized, and choose the symbols needed to notate the pattern by comparing the dictated rhythm with the meter beat.

4. Notate the rhythm that was dictated.

Practice writing the notes and rests in the following four exercises before notating dictation exercises 4.34 through 4.36.

1. Fill in the blank measures with quarter notes and quarter rests.

2. Fill in the blank measures with half notes and half rests.

3. Fill in the blank measures with eighth notes.

4. Fill in the blank measures with sixteenth notes.

Listen to rhythm dictation exercises 4.34, 4.35, and 4.36, then notate them below. The following note values will be used:

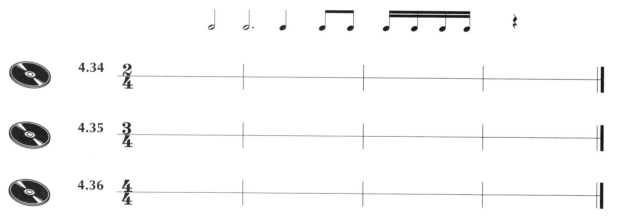

These exercises are notated in Appendix H so that you can check your notation.[1]

---

[1]Additional rhythm dictation exercises can be found in Appendix D, Rhythms for Dictation. Your teacher will play some of these rhythm dictation exercises for you. You may also make your own tape recording of these exercises and play them back so that you can practice memorizing and notating them.

ASSIGNMENT

1. Practice writing the following rhythm notation symbols.

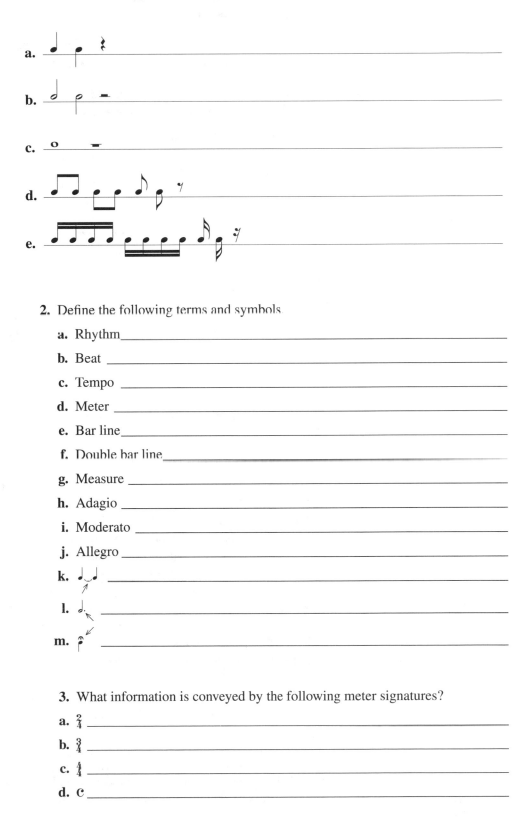

a.

b.

c.

d.

e.

2. Define the following terms and symbols.

a. Rhythm_____

b. Beat _____

c. Tempo _____

d. Meter _____

e. Bar line_____

f. Double bar line_____

g. Measure _____

h. Adagio _____

i. Moderato _____

j. Allegro _____

k. _____

l. _____

m. _____

3. What information is conveyed by the following meter signatures?

a. $\frac{2}{4}$ _____

b. $\frac{3}{4}$ _____

c. $\frac{4}{4}$ _____

d. $\mathbf{c}$ _____

4. Place the proper single and double bar lines in the following rhythm examples, then perform the exercises.

5. Write rhythm syllables above the notes in the following exercises. Also write the meter-beat numbers below the rhythms; indicate the primary and secondary accents with larger numbers (see Chapter 2).

a. Rhythm syllables:

Meter beats:
(numbers)

b. Rhythm syllables:

Meter beats:

c. Rhythm syllables:

Meter beats:

6. Perform rhythm exercises 5a, b, and c: Sing them, and then play them on a keyboard instrument.

7. Practice performing the rhythm studies notated in Appendixes A and C: Sing them, and then play them on a keyboard instrument.

8. Practice improvising rhythms in ⅔, ¾, and ⁴⁄₄ meters until you feel comfortable creating spontaneous short rhythm pieces.

9. Create, notate, and perform a rhythm piece in ⅔, ¾, or ⁴⁄₄ meter. Your composition should be eight measures to sixteen measures in length. Use rhythm pieces 4.26 through 4.33 (pages 28–29) as models for your piece. Use the following procedure to compose your piece.

    a. Decide upon a tempo and a meter that will express the character or feeling you have in mind for your piece.

    b. Choose rhythms from those you have already studied.

    c. Use at least three different rhythms in your piece.

    d. Improvise rhythm patterns on the piano, using the pitch G above the basic beat played on middle C. Next, use the patterns you find most interesting to compose your piece. Follow one rhythmic pattern with another in a musical dialogue, and remember to use repeated and contrasting ideas to create rhythmic phrases that give your piece good form.

e. Review the rhythm dictation procedure presented in this chapter; then notate the rhythm piece you created above the lines provided at the end of this chapter, and notate the meter beats below the lines.

f. Perform the rhythm piece you have created by playing the pitch G above middle C with your right hand as you play the meter beats on middle C with your left hand.

g. After performing your piece several times, decide where different volume levels can be used to make the piece more expressive. Notate these dynamic levels below your manuscript using the following markings: $\boldsymbol{f}$, loud; $\boldsymbol{p}$, soft; ◁———, crescendo; ———▷, diminuendo. Keep in mind that once you introduce a dynamic marking, the music continues at that volume until you introduce a different dynamic marking.

h. Rehearse your piece. If you have trouble performing the two parts simultaneously, find someone to be your performance partner. You should perform the rhythm you created, and your partner should perform the meter beats.

i. Perform your piece for your classmates, friends, or family.

ORIGINAL RHYTHMIC COMPOSITION

Notate your rhythm piece
above the line and perform
on G above middle C.

Notate the meter beats
below the line and perform
on middle C.

chapter 5

Pitch Notation and Performance

PITCH NOTATION

The high–low movement of pitch is indicated by writing the rhythm notation for each pitch on a series of parallel lines and spaces called a **staff** or a **stave.** The staff is formed by five lines and four spaces, which are numbered from the bottom up.

Staff

The note head is placed on a staff line or in a space. The higher the placement, the higher the pitch it represents. Notice that on or below the middle line the stem goes up on the right side of the note head; on or above the middle line the stem goes down on the left side of the note head.

Each staff line and space represents a different pitch (letter). The pitch names are indicated by a **clef sign** placed at the left of each stave.

The lower part of the **G-clef** sign curves around the second line of the staff, indicating that this line represents the pitch G above middle C. This clef is also called the **treble clef** (high clef) because its pitches are above middle C. The G-clef is used to notate music for voices and instruments with ranges in the high register.

G-Clef, or Treble Clef

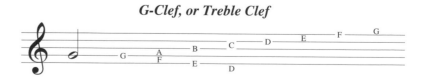

The **F-clef** sign begins on the fourth line of the staff and includes two dots—one placed on each side of the line that represents the pitch F below middle C. This clef is also called the **bass clef** (low clef) because its pitches are below middle C. The F-clef is used to notate music for voices and instruments with ranges in the low register.

F-Clef, or Bass Clef

Ledger lines are short lines that are added for each pitch that needs to be written higher or lower than the five lines of the staff.

Ledger Lines

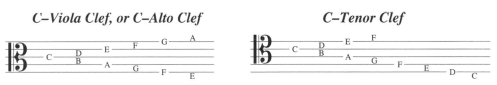

The G-clef and the F-clef are often combined to notate music for instruments with wide ranges—piano, organ, and others. The eleven-line staff that results is called the **grand staff** or the **great staff.**

Grand Staff or Great Staff

The middle line (middle C) is added as a ledger line only when needed.

The **C-clef** consists of two curved lines that join on the staff line representing the pitch middle C. It is a movable clef sign, and although the clef always indicates the line that represents middle C, the C line can be found in different places on the staff. The two most widely used C-clefs are notated here. Study them and notice their relationships to the grand staff.

C–Viola Clef, or C–Alto Clef

The viola clef is used to notate music for the viola, the alto voice of the string instrument family.

C–Tenor Clef

The tenor clef is used occasionally to help eliminate the use of many ledger lines in notated music for cello, trombone, and bassoon.

C–viola clef   C–tenor clef

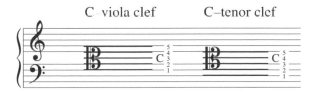

Bar lines and measures, already introduced in our study of rhythm, look like the following when placed on a staff.

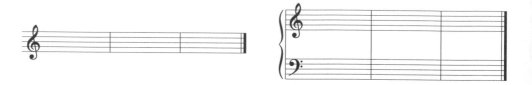

NOTATION OF THE TWELVE-TONE PITCH SYSTEM

Study the following illustration, which shows the notation of the twelve pitches, a half step apart, in two different octaves. Notice the notation of the enharmonic pitches (C♯, D♭; D♯, E♭; etc.). Although they do not appear in the notation here, B can be sharped to sound enharmonically with C, and C can be flatted to sound enharmonically with B; E can be sharped and F can be flatted to sound enharmonically with each other. These enharmonic spellings do not appear in this example because the natural pitches B to C and E to F sound a half step apart.

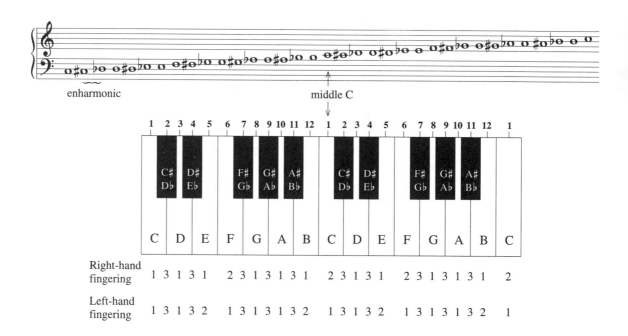

PERFORMING PITCH NOTATION

In Chapter 3 you practiced singing and playing on the piano the pitches C, D, E, F, and G. These pitches are notated in examples 5.1 and 5.2. Listen to each example as you follow the notation, and observe the relationship of each pitch to the illustration of the piano keyboard.

5.1   Play with the left hand.   **5.2**   Play with the right hand.

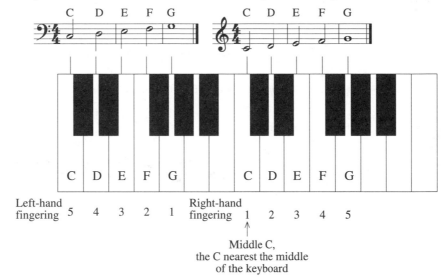

Example 5.2 is notated in the treble clef; it begins with middle C and sounds higher than example 5.1, which begins on the first C below middle C. The treble-clef example represents the pitch sequence C, D, E, F, G in a register comfortable for high-pitched voices and instruments; the bass-clef example, 5.1, represents the same pitch sequence but in the register an octave lower, one that is comfortable for lower-pitched voices and instruments. Listen to these examples again; then perform them on the piano. Next, sing examples 5.1 and 5.2, reciting the letter name of each pitch as if the letters were the words of a song. Because the treble-clef example is higher than the range of most men's voices, men must transpose (transfer) example 5.2 down an octave to sound like example 5.1; and because the bass-clef example is lower than the range of most women's voices, women must transpose example 5.1 up an octave to sound like example 5.2. Learn to read music notated in both clefs, and when necessary, make the appropriate register change when singing.

After you have gained some skill reading exercises 5.1 and 5.2, learn to hear and perform exercises 5.3 through 5.18. These exercises are notated pitch drills similar to the ones you learned to perform in Chapter 3 (exercises 3.1–3.8); they use the first five pitches of the C major scale (C, D, E, F, G), the C major triad (C, E, G), and three of the four pitches of the G dominant seventh chord (G, F, D). As you practice the exercises, learn to hear the five pitches in both scale and chord patterns. Notice that they include the use of the repeat sign. The **repeat sign** :‖ indicates that the previous measures are to be repeated once without stopping the flow of the performance. Use the following procedure.

1. Play each exercise on the piano several times. As you play, memorize the following: the sound of each pitch, its relationship to the scale, its relationship to the chord, the duration of its sound, and its relationship to the beat. Memorize these sounds as you would a recorded song you wanted to sing. Perform the exercises with the metronome ticking and your foot tapping a steady beat (M.M. 60).

2. Sing each exercise as you play it on the piano. Practice until you can sing it in time (with the beat) and in tune.

3. Give yourself only the sound of the first pitch from the piano. Then sing each exercise without playing the piano.

5.3   C scale pattern

M.M. 60

R.H.   1   2   3   4   5

*Repeat sign. Repeat music from the beginning without stopping.

5.4   C scale pattern

R.H.   1 2 3 4   5

5.5   C major triad—chord pattern

R.H.   1   3   5

5.6   C major triad—chord pattern

R.H.   1   3   5

5.7   C major triad—chord pattern (3rd omitted)

R.H.   1   5   1

5.8   Scale pattern and chord pattern

R.H.   1   2   3

5.9   G dominant 7th—chord pattern

R.H.   5   4   2   5   1   5   1

5.10 G dominant 7th—chord pattern

R.H. 5 4

5.11 C scale pattern

L.H. 5 4 3 2 1

5.12 C scale pattern

L.H. 5 4 3 2 1

5.13 C major triad—chord pattern

L.H. 5 3 1

5.14 C major triad—chord pattern

L.H. 5 3 1

5.15 C major triad—chord pattern (3rd omitted)

L.H. 5 1 5

5.16 Scale pattern and chord pattern

L.H. 5 4 3

5.17   G dominant 7th—chord pattern

L.H.   1   2   4   1   5   1   5

5.18   G dominant 7th—chord pattern

L.H.   1   2

IMPROVE YOUR NOTATION-READING SKILLS

Having studied, performed, and memorized the sound of scale and chord patterns that use the first five pitches of the C major scale, you are ready to play and sing notated melodic exercises 5.19–5.34, which use these pitches. Chord symbols have been notated above each exercise to help you recognize the scale/chord relationship of the pitches in each measure. Use the following procedure.

1. Play each exercise on the piano several times. As you play, memorize the following: the sound of each pitch, its relationship to the scale, its relationship to the chord, the duration of its sound, and its relationship to the beat. Memorize these sounds as you would a recorded song you wanted to sing. Perform the exercises with the metronome ticking and your foot tapping a steady beat.

2. Sing each exercise as you play it on the piano. Practice until you can sing it in time (with the beat) and in tune.

3. Give yourself only the sound of the first pitch from the piano. Then sing each exercise without playing the piano.

For additional melodic exercises, see Appendix E, Melodic Studies.

5.19   M.M. 86

5.20   M.M. 86

MELODIC DICTATION

In addition to developing the ability to translate pitch notation into sound, you must develop the skills for translating melodic sounds into notation. This process, the opposite of reading notation, is referred to as taking **melodic dictation;** it is an essential part of music studies designed to improve your aural perception.

Use the following procedure when notating dictated melodies.

1. The pitch series (scale or part of a scale) used to create the melody will be notated in the text and performed. Memorize the sound and relationship of each pitch in the pitch series when it is performed on the recording or by the person playing the dictated melody.

2. Notice the clef sign, the meter signature, and the starting pitch. All are notated in the text.

3. Tap your foot silently so that you can feel the basic beat and the meter when the tempo is given on the recording or by the person playing the dictated melody.

4. Listen to the dictated melody and memorize it.

5. To identify the exact pitch of each melody note, repeat the melodic idea in your mind and compare the pitches of the melody with the pitch series you have memorized.

6. Notate the pitches dictated by placing small dots on the proper lines and spaces of the staff.

7. Choose the rhythm symbols needed for notating the dictated melody by comparing the length of the rhythms heard with the basic beat you feel as you tap your foot. This is the same process as taking rhythm dictation.

8. When you decide upon the rhythm symbol for each of the pitches, change the pitch dot into a note head; add a note stem and a beam or a flag if needed. Then add bar lines to complete the notation of the dictated melody. As you become more skilled at taking melodic dictation, you will be able to perceive and notate pitch and rhythm in one step, combining steps 5, 6, 7, and 8.

Listen to and study recorded example 5.35. This example demonstrates the step-by-step process for notating dictated melodies.

5.35   The pitch series to be memorized.   The dictated melodic idea. When writing other dictation exercises, you will hear but not see the dictated melody.

1. Memorize the dictated melodic idea. Clef sign, time signature, and starting pitch are given.

2. Notate pitches with dots.

3. Change pitch dots into rhythm notation.

4. Add bar lines.

Play each of the recorded dictation exercises (5.36–5.41) several times, and notate each exercise on the staff provided. Use the dictation procedures suggested in example 5.35. These exercises are notated in Appendix H so that you can check your notation.[1]

    5.36   *Pitch series:*

Notate three-measure melodic idea here.

    5.37   *Pitch series:*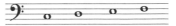

Notate two-measure melodic idea here.

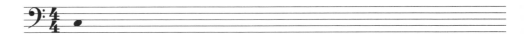

    5.38   *Pitch series:*

Notate three-measure melodic idea here.

    5.39   *Pitch series:*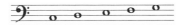

Notate three-measure melodic idea here.

[1]Additional melodic dictation exercises can be found in Appendix F, Melodies for Dictation. Your teacher will play some of these melodic dictation exercises for you. You may also make your own tape recording of these exercises and play them back so that you can practice memorizing and notating them.

5.40 *Pitch series:*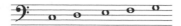

Notate six-measure melody here.

 5.41 *Pitch series:*

Notate eight-measure melody here.

MELODY CONSTRUCTION

Your study of melody began with the song *Just Sing It!* (example 1.1). By listening to and performing this piece, you have come to understand that a melody is the shortest complete musical expression. You have also studied the smaller parts of a melody that make up the whole: the phrase, a natural division of the melodic line, comparable to a sentence and ending with a cadence (resting point); and the period, two phrases working together in a question-answer relationship, the first phrase (antecedent phrase) giving the impression that more is to come, and the second phrase (consequent phrase) completing the musical statement. The period may be likened to a compound sentence.

The smallest melodic fragment is called a **motive.** It is the most brief, intelligible, and self-contained melodic or rhythmic fragment; it may be likened to a short clause within the sentence structure. The motive, the smallest "building block" of music, may be used to construct phrases, phrases used to construct periods, periods used to construct melodies, and melodies used to construct larger musical works.

Form in music—within the phrase, the melody, or the larger work—is created by the interaction of repeated musical fragments and new, contrasting musical ideas. Three types of repetition are used extensively: **exact repetition,** in which a melodic or a rhythmic idea is repeated exactly as first presented; **sequential repetition,** or **sequence,** in which a melodic idea is repeated but at a different pitch level; and **varied repetition,** in which the motive is slightly varied rhythmically or melodically but is still recognizable.

Musical **contrast** refers to new material introduced to offer the needed relief from repeated material. The form of most musical compositions can be thought of in relationship to the balance between repetition and contrast. Too much repetition becomes boring, and continuous contrast without some melodic or rhythmic repetition can lead to incoherent musical expressions.

Study, listen to, and perform example 5.42. This melodic example will help you understand the use of motives, phrases, and periods. It will also serve to acquaint you with the techniques of melodic and rhythmic repetition, sequence, varied repetition, and contrast as they apply to the art of composing a melody.

5.42

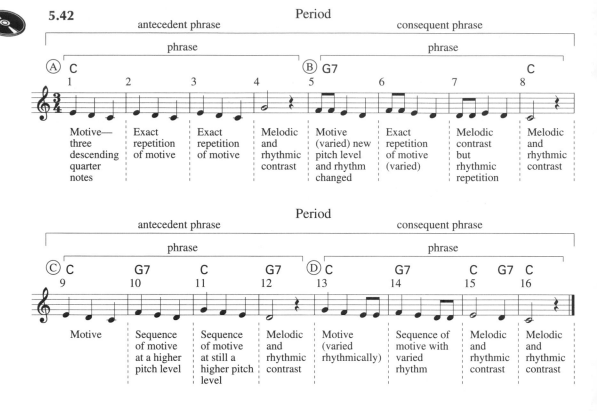

To increase your understanding of melodic and rhythmic repetition, sequence, varied repetition, and contrast, listen to the first movement of Symphony No. 5 by Ludwig van Beethoven. The opening motive, notated here, supplies both melodic and rhythmic material for the structure of the entire movement.[2]

ASSIGNMENT

1. Define the following terms.

    a. Pitch _____

    b. Melody _____

    c. Sequence _____

    d. Phrase _____

    e. Period _____

    f. Cadence _____

[2]A recording of this symphony should be available in your school or public library.

2. Name and define:

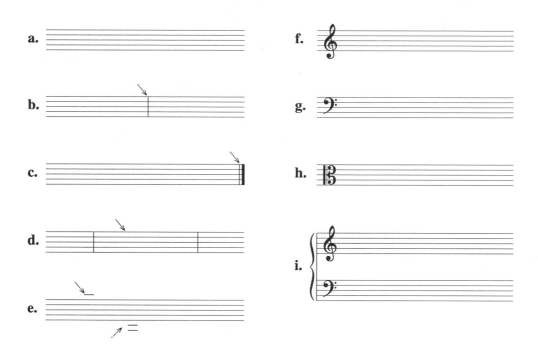

3. Identify the following pitches by writing the letter name below each note.

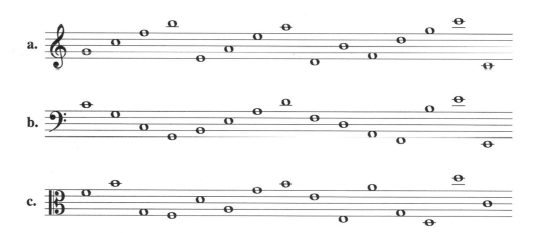

4. Perform each of the following exercises after writing the rhythm syllables above the notation.

5. Practice performing rhythm studies notated in Appendixes A and C, and melodic studies notated in Appendix E. Sing these exercises and play them on a keyboard instrument.

6. Practice improvising short melodies on the piano. Use the pitches C, D, E, F, and G and various meters and tempos. Structure your melodies by using exact and sequential repetition, and contrasting melodic and rhythmic ideas. Hear the five-pitch scale/chord patterns in your mind as you improvise, and *play only what you hear.* Don't just move your fingers up and down the keyboard. Use changing dynamics to make your pieces more expressive.

7. Create, notate, and perform a sixteen-measure melody using only the pitches C, D, E, F, and G. Use the following procedures, and study example 5.42 (page 46) as a model for your melody.

   a. Decide upon a tempo and a meter that will help express the character you have in mind for your melody.

   b. Use all five pitches (C, D, E, F, and G) and a variety of rhythms (at least three different note values ♩ ♫ ♩) to create your melody.

   c. Improvise one phrase at a time; remember to use repeated, sequential, and contrasting musical ideas to give your phrases form. Hear the five-pitch scale/chord patterns in your mind as you improvise, and use scale and chord movement of pitches as you create your melodic ideas.

   d. Choose the best melodic ideas that you have improvised to construct four phrases that work together as two periods (see example 5.42, page 46). This will give your sixteen-measure melody good form. Remember that your melodic ideas should work together to make a musical statement and that the beat is the glue that holds your piece together.

   e. Notate your melody on the staves provided at the end of this chapter. Follow the same procedure you used for notating dictated melodies, and add appropriate tempo and dynamic markings to convey the expressive qualities of your composition.

   f. Practice performing your melody on the piano.

   g. Perform your melody for friends or classmates.

Although there is no such thing as a correct or an incorrect melody, the rhythms and pitches you choose should be properly notated, your manuscript legible, and your performance well prepared.

ORIGINAL MELODY NO. 1 USING PITCHES C–G

chapter 6

Scales

SCALES

A **scale** is a series of pitches that are related, one to the other, both melodically and harmonically. There are many scale types, and each of these pitch systems may be thought of as a series of ascending or descending pitches. Each scale has an unchanging pitch pattern and a unique, characteristic sound. Since scales are basic to the organization of pitch in music, it is important to develop an understanding of the many scale types and their unique expressive qualities.

Although this text will focus mainly on the study of major and minor scales, a wide variety of scales will be presented in this chapter. All will be constructed on the pitch C to make both visual and sound comparisons easier. As you study, keep in mind that *all scale types can be constructed on any of the twelve tones.* Information regarding the transposition (transfer) of scales to all twelve pitches will conclude this chapter.

DIATONIC SCALES

Diatonic scales have eight tones and extend from a given pitch to its octave, ascending or descending. They use all seven pitches of the musical alphabet—A, B, C, D, E, F, G—in a pattern that includes five **whole tones** (whole steps) and two **semitones** (half steps). There are only seven diatonic scales, and they can be produced by playing the white keys of the piano (C–C, D–D, E–E, F–F, G–G, A–A, B–B). Play these seven scales and notice that the half steps between B and C and between E and F appear in different places in each scale, depending upon which note begins the scale. Also notice that each scale sounds unique because the placement of the half steps and whole steps within each scale is different. These seven natural (white keys only) diatonic scales include modal, major, and minor scales, and all seven may be transposed (transferred) to begin on any of the twelve tones (natural, sharp, or flat pitches).

Modal Scales

The earliest diatonic scales date back to the middle ages (fifth century–fifteenth century) and were called **modes.** Because they were used in church music of that time, they are often referred to as **church modes.**

The seven church modes when played on the white keys are the same as the natural diatonic scales you just played. They are named **ionian,** C–C; **dorian,** D–D; **phrygian,** E–E; **lydian,** F–F; **mixolydian,** G–G; **aeolian,** A–A; and **locrian,** B–B. For easier visual and sound comparison, these modes are written in examples 6.1–6.7 beginning on the pitch C. Visual symbols above and below the notation indicate the whole-step and half-step intervals between the pitches of each mode: ⌒ = whole step, ⌄ = half step. These symbols are used as teaching aids and are not a part of music notation. Study, then sing and play the following modes on the piano, using the fingerings written below each example. Use the keyboard illustration to help you find the pitches on your instrument.

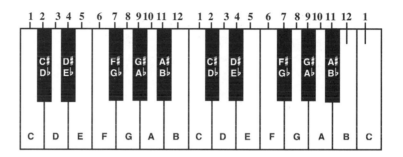

6.1 C ionian (same as C major scale)

R.H. 1   2   3   1   2   3   4   5

6.2 C dorian

1   2   3   1   2   3   4   5

6.3 C phrygian

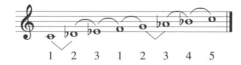

1   2   3   1   2   3   4   5

6.4 C lydian

1   2   3   4   1   2   3   4

6.5   C mixolydian

1   2   3   1   2   3   4   5

6.6   C aeolian (same as C natural minor scale)

1   2   3   1   2   3   4   5

6.7   C locrian

1   2   3   1   2   3   4   5

Equal Temperament and the Major/Minor Tonal System

About the mid–seventeenth century two important practices developed that changed the approach to making music. These practices, and the changes they brought about, are still used today.

The first change was a new method of tuning in which the octave was divided into twelve equal half steps. This method of tuning was called **equal temperament,** and although all pitches except the octave were slightly incorrect in relationship to nature's acoustics, this method offered important advantages over other systems of tuning. First, it established the same sound for all enharmonic pitches (e.g., G-sharp and A-flat sound the same). That in turn made it possible to transpose a piece of music based on a given scale from one pitch to a different pitch and retain the melodic and harmonic sound of the original piece. **Just intonation** (a system of natural acoustical tuning) and other tuning methods did not allow for transposition without changing the original sound.

The second change was an increasing preference by musicians for the use of major and minor scales over the use of modal scales and the practices associated with the church modes. By the mid–eighteenth century major and minor scales had become the predominant approach to pitch organization in Western music. It was the application of these two scales, and the harmonic and melodic practices associated with them, to the equal temperament tuning that brought about the development of the **major/minor tonal system.** This system of melodic and harmonic interaction between major and minor scales constructed on all of the twelve pitches greatly expanded the melodic and harmonic possibilities of music.

The Major Scale

The **major scale** is a series of eight diatonic pitches arranged in an unchanging pattern of whole step, whole step, half step, whole step, whole step, whole step, half step. The half steps are located between scale degrees 3 and 4, and 7 and 1 (the octave). This scale extends from a given pitch to its octave and is performed with the same pitches both ascending and descending.

Study the C major scale notated in example 6.8. Next, sing and play the C major scale on the keyboard. You will recognize the sound of this scale; it was used in *Just Sing It!* (example 1.3). As you perform, *memorize* the sound of this scale and the whole-step and half-step intervals between the eight pitches. Use the fingering written below the example.

6.8   C major scale

Scale degrees:	1	2	3	4	5	6	7	1
Right-hand fingering:	1	2	3	1	2	3	4	5
Left-hand fingering:	5	4	3	2	1	3	2	1

Minor Scales

There are three forms of the minor scale—natural minor, melodic minor, and harmonic minor—and all three forms can be related to the major scale. Because major and minor scales are related and function together melodically and harmonically within the major/minor tonal system, it is best to study minor scales through their relationship to the major scale rather than as separate scales. In this chapter minor scales are introduced as color variations of the major scale, making the aural and visual recognition of their relationship easier.

The Natural Minor Scale   Study the C major and C natural minor scales notated in example 6.9. Like the major scale, the **natural minor scale** extends from a given pitch to its octave, uses the seven diatonic scale degrees, and is performed with the same pitches ascending and descending. In the natural minor scale, however, the third, sixth, and seventh scale degrees have been lowered one half step from the major to create its unique minor sound. Notice that lowering these three pitches places the half steps between scale degrees 2 and 3, and 5 and 6. These two C scales start on the same pitch, and their relationship is referred to as **parallel major and minor.**

After studying these two scales, sing them and play them on the keyboard. *Memorize* the sound of each scale and the differences and likenesses that exist between them.

6.9

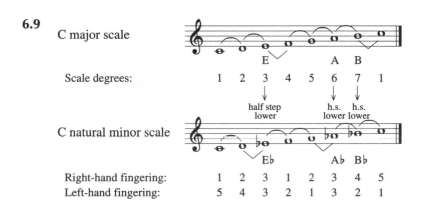

Right-hand fingering:	1	2	3	1	2	3	4	5
Left-hand fingering:	5	4	3	2	1	3	2	1

The Melodic Minor Scale   For a greater choice of melodic pitches, composers often use the sixth and seventh scale degrees of the parallel major scale with the lowered third scale degree of the natural minor to create another form of the minor scale. This scale is generally used in conjunction with the natural minor scale form, and because it evolved from melodic considerations, it is called the **melodic minor scale.** For convenience of analysis, this scale is written ascending with the third scale degree lowered one half step from the parallel major, and descending as a natural minor scale, with the third, sixth, and seventh scale degrees lowered one half step from the parallel major.

Study, then sing and play on the keyboard the C major and C melodic minor scales notated in example 6.10. Notice that the ascending melodic minor scale sounds like the parallel major, except for the lowered third scale degree; and the descending melodic minor scale sounds like the natural minor scale. Compare the whole-step and half-step patterns of these two scales, and then *memorize* the sound of each scale and the differences and likenesses that exist between them.

6.10

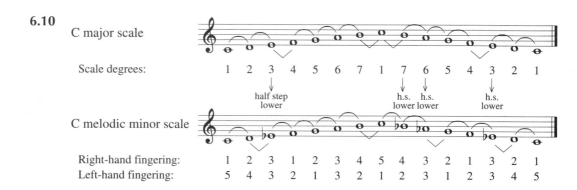

By using the melodic minor scale, the composer has a choice between the major and minor sixth and seventh scale degrees. Although in the melodic minor scale the sixth and seventh scale degrees are raised ascending and lowered descending, there is no rule that says that in music compositions these scale degrees must be raised ascending and lowered descending. Sometimes they are, and sometimes they are not; it is the composer's choice.

The Harmonic Minor Scale   The third minor scale form is constructed from the three primary harmonies of the minor scale, and it, too, can be related to the parallel major scale. This scale is called the **harmonic minor scale** because its primary function within the major/minor tonal system is harmonic. The harmonic minor scale, like the parallel major scale, extends from a given pitch to its octave, uses the seven diatonic scale degrees, and is performed with the same pitches ascending and descending. In the harmonic minor scale, however, the third and sixth scale degrees are lowered one half step from the parallel major to create its unique minor sound. Study the whole-step, half-step sequence and notice that this scale has three whole steps, three half steps, and a one-and-a-half step interval between scale degrees 6 and 7. This unique pattern makes the harmonic minor scale an altered diatonic scale.

Study, then sing and play on the keyboard the C major and C harmonic minor scales notated in example 6.11. *Memorize* the sound of each scale and the differences and likenesses that exist between them.

6.11

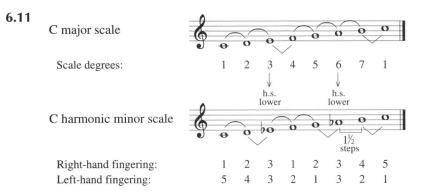

C major scale

Scale degrees: 1   2   3   4   5   6   7   1

h.s. lower   h.s. lower

C harmonic minor scale

1½ steps

Right-hand fingering: 1   2   3   1   2   3   4   5
Left-hand fingering: 5   4   3   2   1   3   2   1

The Gypsy Scale

The **Gypsy scale,** also known as the **Hungarian scale,** is closely related in sound to the harmonic minor scale. Except for the raised fourth scale degree, the pitches of the Gypsy scale are identical to those of the harmonic minor scale. The raised fourth scale degree, however, creates a very different interval pattern: one whole step, four half steps, and two step-and-a-half intervals. Like the harmonic minor scale, the Gypsy scale is an altered diatonic scale.

Study, then sing and play the two scales notated in example 6.12. *Memorize* the sound of each scale and the differences and likenesses that exist between them.

6.12

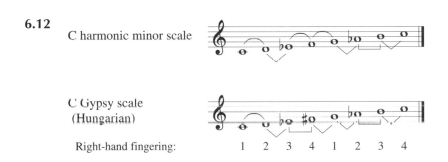

C harmonic minor scale

C Gypsy scale
(Hungarian)

Right-hand fingering: 1   2   3   4   1   2   3   4

MAJOR AND MINOR PENTATONIC SCALES

Pentatonic denotes any five-note scale, and there are many pentatonic scale patterns. The major and minor pentatonic scales notated in example 6.13 are similar to the major and natural minor scales, except that the diatonic pitches that create the half-step intervals in the major and minor scales have been eliminated. These and other pentatonic scales have played a significant role in both Western and non-Western music for centuries.

Study, then sing and play on the keyboard the following major and minor pentatonic scales. *Memorize* the sound of these important pentatonic sales.

6.13

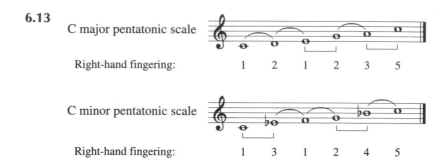

C major pentatonic scale

Right-hand fingering: 1   2   1   2   3   5

C minor pentatonic scale

Right-hand fingering: 1   3   1   2   4   5

BLUES SCALES

Like the pentatonic scale, the **blues scale** exists in many patterns. The common feature of all blues scales is the use of the flatted third, fifth, and seventh scale degrees when compared with the parallel major scale. Blues scales are associated with music performed in the blues and jazz styles and with compositions influenced by those styles.

Study, then sing and play the blues scale notated in example 6.14. Notice that this blues scale uses the pitches of the minor pentatonic scale with an additional scale degree, the flatted fifth (enharmonic sharped fourth). *Memorize* the sound of this blues scale.

6.14

C blues scale

Right-hand fingering: 1   3   1   3   1   3   4

SYNTHETIC SCALES

Any group of pitches can be arranged in a unique sequence and called a scale. The scales termed **synthetic, hybrid,** or **artificial** are designed for special uses and are limited in number and variety only by the composer's imagination. Four synthetic scales used widely in the twentieth century will be presented in this chapter. All four of these scale types are **symmetrical scales** (scales constructed with a series of identical intervals). They are the chromatic, whole-tone, augmented, and diminished scales.

The Chromatic Scale

When all twelve pitches are played ascending or descending in a half-step sequence, they form a **chromatic scale.** The chromatic scale is the most common symmetrical scale, and because it contains only half steps it is easy to recognize. This scale is usually notated with sharps when ascending and flats when descending. Study, then play the chromatic scale notated in example 6.15. *Memorize* the sound of its half-step sequence and the method used for notating it.

6.15   C chromatic scale (half-step interval between pitches)

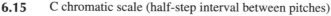

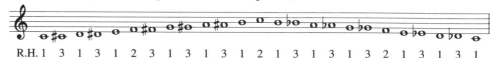

R.H. 1   3   1   3   1   2   3   1   3   1   3   1   3   1   2   1   3   1   3   1   3   1   3   2   1   3   1   3   1

Chromaticism **Chromaticism,** movement by half step between the pitches of the diatonic scale, began to be used in melodies, and to a lesser degree harmonies, in the mid–sixteenth century. These chromatic pitches were used to add color to the overall modal sound of the music. When the major/minor tonal system became the primary method of pitch organization in the seventeenth century, chromatic pitches continued to be used to color the melodies and harmonies of pieces using this system. Use of chromaticism in music increased through the eighteenth and nineteenth centuries, until, in the early twentieth century, some music used all twelve tones to organize pitch content without reference to major, minor, or modal scales. These pieces used the chromatic scale as a tonal province in its own right.

Be aware that diatonic semitones (half-step intervals involving a change of pitch degree—e.g., E–F, C–D-flat) and chromatic semitones (half-step intervals involving the same pitch degree—e.g., C–C-sharp, A-flat–A) affect the scale differently. Both the lower and the upper pitches of the diatonic semitone are a part of the scale and its characteristic melodic and harmonic sounds. One of the two pitches of the chromatic semitone is not a part of the scale. This chromatic pitch, therefore, changes or adds color to the music when it is interjected into a piece that uses a particular scale that does not include the chromatic tone.

The Whole-Tone Scale

The **whole-tone scale** extends from a given pitch to its octave, but it uses only six of the seven diatonic pitches; all pitches are a whole step apart. The unique whole-step sound of this symmetrical scale is as easily recognized as the half-step sound of the chromatic scale.

Study, then sing and play the whole-tone scale notated in example 6.16. *Memorize* the sound of this scale.

6.16 C whole-tone scale (whole-step interval between pitches)

Right-hand fingering: 1   2   1   2   3   4   5

The Augmented Scale

The **augmented scale,** also called the **minor third–half-step scale,** is constructed in a symmetrical pattern of consecutive minor third (one-and-a-half steps) and half-step intervals. Like the whole-tone scale, it uses only six of the diatonic scale degrees before the first pitch of the scale is repeated at the octave.

Study, then sing and play the augmented scale notated in example 6.17. *Memorize* the sound of this scale.

6.17 C augmented scale

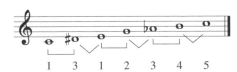

Right-hand fingering: 1   3   1   2   3   4   5

Diminished Scales

The **diminished scale,** also known as the **octatonic scale,** is constructed with a symmetrical pattern that alternates whole steps and half steps. This scale extends from a given pitch to its octave, but it contains eight different pitches. Because the diminished scale contains eight pitches, one of the diatonic pitches is repeated, but with a different accidental. The choice of the repeated pitch used to spell this scale may vary.

There are two forms of the diminished scale, one that begins with a whole-step interval and one that is referred to as the **inverted diminished scale,** which begins with a half-step interval.

Study, then sing and play the diminished scales notated in example 6.18. *Memorize* the sound of each scale.

6.18

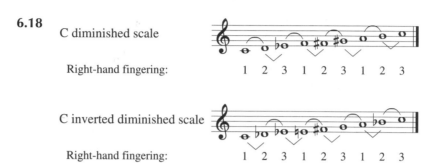

TONAL CENTER

Throughout the evolution of music—in all periods and cultures, and regardless of style—nearly every piece of music has given preference to one of its pitches. This melodic and harmonic preference for one tone creates a **tonal center** to which all other pitches are related.

The only exception to this universal preference for a tonal center occurs in twentieth-century atonal music. **Atonal music** purposely avoids creating a tonal center in an effort to give all twelve pitches equal influence in the overall piece. This practice was most prevalent during the early part of the twentieth century, when much experimentation in music composition occurred. Following this brief experimental stage, composers have returned almost completely to writing music with a tonal center.

TONALITY AND KEY

The first pitch of a major or a minor scale, called the **tonic** or the **keynote,** serves as the tonal center of the scale. **Tonality** and **key** are synonymous terms used to refer to the loyalty of a major or a minor piece of music to the tonic (keynote) of the scale used to organize its pitch content. For example, a composition using the scale of C minor is said to have the tonality of C minor or to be in the key of C minor.

MODALITY

It is common to think of **modality** as the tonal center of a church mode, and tonality as the tonal center of a major or a minor scale. Modality, however, is often used in a broader sense to encompass all scale-type possibilities on a given pitch. It could, therefore, be said that tonality, or key, can exist in different "modal" varieties based upon all scale types. For example, pieces written with a tonal center on the pitch C but with different scale/mode types may be referred to as being in the following modes.

Key of

C major mode

C minor mode (natural, harmonic, or melodic form)

C pentatonic mode (major or minor form)

C dorian mode

C chromatic mode

C whole-tone mode

C any synthetic mode

TRANSPOSING SCALES TO DIFFERENT KEYNOTES

All scale types can be constructed on any of the twelve tones. One keynote may be chosen over another to accommodate voice or instrument ranges. For example, if you were unable to sing the lowest pitch of a melody in the key of C major, you would need to transpose (transfer) the piece up to the key of D major or maybe E major to be sure the lowest pitch was within your range. Different keys are also used to avoid the monotony of sound caused by using the same tonal center over and over. If you attended a concert and the first four pieces were all in the key of D major, you would grow tired of the repetition of pitches and would welcome a change of key.

To construct a particular scale on any pitch, select a keynote and then use the unique interval pattern that exists between the pitches of the scale you are writing to determine the remaining pitches (e.g., D, whole step to E, half step to F). To achieve the proper placement of whole steps and half steps within the scale, you may have to use accidentals (sharps or flats) to alter natural pitches. For example, if a whole step is needed above the pitch E to achieve the correct scale sequence, an F-sharp would be used; if a half step is needed above the pitch D, then an E-flat would be used. See the following examples.

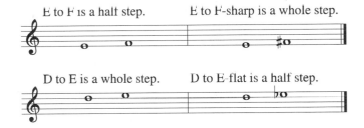

ASSIGNMENT

1. Add the necessary sharps or flats to construct the following scales. Do this assignment while seated at a keyboard, or see page 51 for a drawing of the chromatic keyboard. After writing these scales, sing them and play them on a keyboard instrument.

   a. E major

b. G natural minor

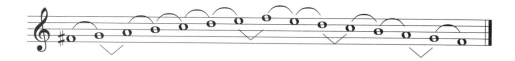

c. F-sharp melodic minor

d. A-flat harmonic minor

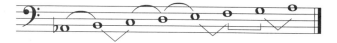

e. F dorian

f. A lydian

g. B mixolydian

h. D major pentatonic

i. B minor pentatonic

j. E Gypsy

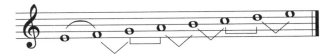

k. G blues

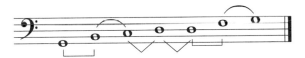

l. D chromatic (all half-step intervals; fill in missing pitches)

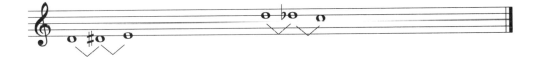

m. A-flat whole-tone

n. D diminished

2. Continue daily performances of rhythm exercises notated in Appendix C, Rhythm Studies. Sing these exercises and play them on a keyboard instrument.

3. Continue improvising rhythm pieces in different meters and various tempos. Sing your improvisations and play them on a keyboard instrument.

4. Continue daily performances of melody exercises notated in Appendix E, Melodic Studies. Sing these exercises and play them on a keyboard instrument.

5. Continue improvising melodies in different meters using the first five pitches of the C major scale (C, D, E, F, G). Begin to improvise melodies based upon some of the scales presented in this chapter that you found interesting (e.g., C major, C harmonic minor, C major pentatonic, C blues). Begin by playing the scale up and down, using the fingering written below the notated scale; do this over and over in time with a steady beat until you can hear and perform the scale well. Then set a tempo and a meter and begin improvising melodies using the complete scale; employ the same techniques you used to improvise and create melodies using only five pitches. Notice that each scale produces melodies that resemble the unique sound of that scale.

chapter 7

Major and Minor Key Signatures

KEY SIGNATURE

Before you perform a notated composition, you should know its key (tonality), for the key identifies the scale tones from which the piece was created. This information will in turn help you hear the pitches and feel the character of the music. If you can hear a particular scale, then you will be able to hear the music that was written using that scale.

To facilitate the identification of the key, and to make the writing and reading of pitch notation easier, the sharps and flats needed to alter the pitches of the scale used to compose a piece are placed at the beginning of each staff following the clef sign. These sharps or flats appear in a specific order and may range in number from one to seven; they are referred to as a **key signature.** Each key signature, depending upon the number of sharps or flats it contains, represents a major or a minor scale; and each sharp or flat appearing in the key signature indicates that that particular pitch (letter) is to be sharped or flatted every time it is used within the piece. The key signature, therefore, makes it easy for the performer to know at a glance the scale that was used to write the composition and the pitches that will be sharped or flatted throughout the piece.

Compare the following examples notated with and without key signatures. Notice that the examples written with key signatures appear less cluttered and are therefore easier to read. Also notice that writing the key signature once on each staff eliminates the necessity to rewrite a sharp or a flat before every note in the piece that should be altered.

Scale and melodic segment in the key of A-flat major: (1) notated without a key signature; (2) notated with a key signature

Scale and melodic segment in the key of G-sharp minor: (1) notated without a key signature; (2) notated with a key signature

EFFECT OF ACCIDENTALS UPON THE KEY SIGNATURE

Sharp (♯), flat (♭), or natural (♮) accidentals may be used within a piece to alter the key signature. When an accidental is notated in the music, it cancels the sharp, flat, or natural in the key signature that it replaces, and its alteration applies to all similar pitches that follow within the same measure. Another accidental, however, may be used within that measure to cancel the previous accidental. Bar lines also cancel previous accidentals and restore the key signature, unless the pitch changed by the accidental is tied over into the next measure, in which case, the accidental is canceled after the tied note has been performed. Study the following example.

A B♭ A B♭   A B♮ B♭B♮ A B♮ B♭   B♭ A B♮ A G♯ A G♯ G♯ F♯ G♮F♮ F♮   F♯ F♯ G

Write the letter names below each pitch of the following melody.

Letters:

IDENTIFYING MAJOR AND MINOR KEYNOTES FROM KEY SIGNATURES

Each key signature represents two scales—a major scale and a minor scale. The key signature, therefore, indicates to the performer two possible tonalities for the music about to be performed, one major and the other minor. At this point you must learn to identify the two possible keys; later in this chapter you will learn which of the two possible keys applies to a particular piece of music.

Memorize the following rules for identifying keynotes from a given key signature, and study the examples presented to illustrate the application of these rules.

A. Sharp Key Signatures

1. Major keys: The last sharp to the right is the seventh scale degree. Count up to the first scale degree; 1 is the keynote.

The last sharp to the right is C-sharp; therefore, the major keynote is D and the scale is D major.

The last sharp to the right is D-sharp; therefore, the major keynote is E and the scale is E major.

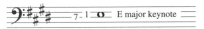

2. Minor keys: The minor keynote is three scale degrees below the major keynote; the minor keynote is the sixth scale degree of the major scale.

The major keynote is D; therefore, the minor keynote is B and the scale is B minor.

The major keynote is E; therefore, the minor keynote is C-sharp and the scale is C-sharp minor.

B. Flat Key Signatures

1. Major keys: The last flat to the right is the fourth scale degree. Count down to the first scale degree; 1 is the keynote. Or if there is more than one flat in the key signature, the next-to-last flat (to the right) is the keynote.

The last flat to the right is B-flat; therefore, the major keynote is F and the scale is F major.

The last flat to the right is E-flat; therefore, the major keynote is B-flat and the scale is B-flat major.

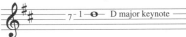

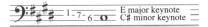

2. Minor keys: The minor keynote is three scale degrees below the major keynote; the minor keynote is the sixth scale degree of the major scale.

The major keynote is F; therefore, the minor keynote is D and the scale is D minor.

The major keynote is B-flat; therefore, the minor keynote is G and the scale is G minor.

Use the rules just given to identify the major and minor keynotes of the following key signatures.

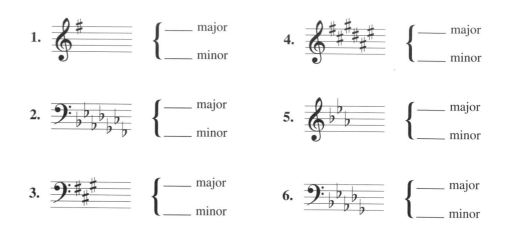

1. _____ major
   _____ minor

2. _____ major
   _____ minor

3. _____ major
   _____ minor

4. _____ major
   _____ minor

5. _____ major
   _____ minor

6. _____ major
   _____ minor

Following are all twelve major and minor key signatures, plus six enharmonic key signatures. These are the thirty key signatures that you will encounter again and again in notated music. *Memorize* the key signatures and their keynotes by practicing this drill: Cover the keynote letters with a piece of paper and practice identifying the major and minor keynotes. Also refer to this chart to check the answers for work you do in this and other chapters.

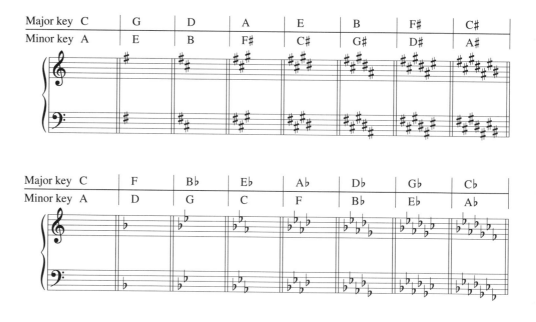

Major key	C	G	D	A	E	B	F♯	C♯
Minor key	A	E	B	F♯	C♯	G♯	D♯	A♯

Major key	C	F	B♭	E♭	A♭	D♭	G♭	C♭
Minor key	A	D	G	C	F	B♭	E♭	A♭

RELATIVE AND PARALLEL MAJOR AND MINOR SCALES

Composers often use major and minor keys within the same piece of music. These major and minor scales may be related to one another by either a common key signature (**relative major, relative minor**) or a common keynote (**parallel major, parallel minor**). Study and *memorize* the following rules regarding relative and parallel major and minor scale relationships.

A. When a major and a minor scale have a common key signature but different keynotes (tonics), the scales are said to be *relative*. Study the following examples. Observe that the keynote of the relative minor scale is the same pitch as the sixth scale degree of the relative major scale—three letters (one-and-a-half steps) below the relative major keynote—and that the keynote of the relative major scale is the same pitch as the third scale degree of the relative minor scale—three letters (one-and-a-half steps) above the relative minor keynote.

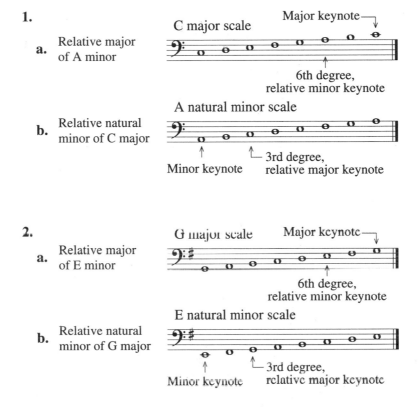

1.
  a. Relative major of A minor
  b. Relative natural minor of C major

2.
  a. Relative major of E minor
  b. Relative natural minor of G major

B. When the same pitch serves as the keynote (tonic) for both a major and a minor scale but the key signatures are different, the scales are said to be *parallel*. Study the following examples. Observe that a major scale becomes a parallel minor scale when the third, sixth, and seventh scale degrees are lowered a half step (the same as adding three flats to a major key signature) and that a minor scale becomes a parallel major scale when the third, sixth, and seventh scale degrees are raised a half step (the same as adding three sharps to a minor key signature). When adding sharps or flats to a key signature, keep in mind that flats cancel sharps and sharps cancel flats.

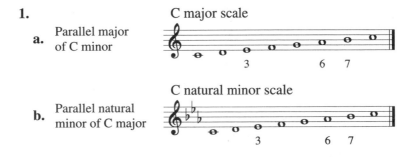

1.
  a. Parallel major of C minor
  b. Parallel natural minor of C major

2.

    a. Parallel major of D minor

D major scale

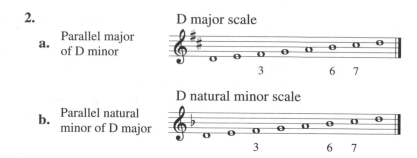

    b. Parallel natural minor of D major

D natural minor scale

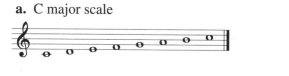

C. All major and minor scales are related to two other scales. Each major scale is related to a relative minor scale by key signature and to a parallel minor scale by keynote. Each minor scale is related to a relative major scale by key signature and to a parallel major scale by keynote. Study the following examples.

1. The C major scale is related to the relative A minor scale and the parallel C minor scale.

    a. C major scale

    b. A natural minor scale   **c.** C natural minor scale

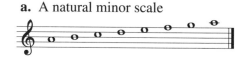

2. The A minor scale is related to the relative C major scale and the parallel A major scale.

    a. A natural minor scale

    b. C major scale   **c.** A major scale

Identify the following scales and their relative or parallel relationship. First, look at each key signature and determine the major and minor keynote it represents. Then study each scale to see if its tonic (first scale degree) is the major or the minor keynote. Finally, compare the keynotes of scales 1 and 2 to determine their relationship.

A.

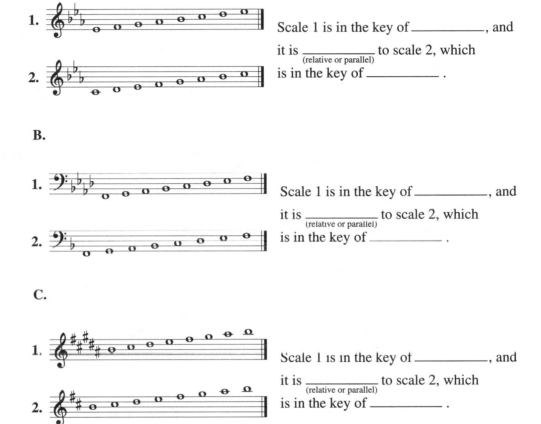

Scale 1 is in the key of _____, and it is _____ to scale 2, which (relative or parallel) is in the key of _____ .

B.

Scale 1 is in the key of _____, and it is _____ to scale 2, which (relative or parallel) is in the key of _____ .

C.

Scale 1 is in the key of _____, and it is _____ to scale 2, which (relative or parallel) is in the key of _____ .

D.

Scale 1 is in the key of _____, and it is _____ to scale 2, which (relative or parallel) is in the key of _____ .

Musical Examples of Relative and Parallel Key Relationships

Composers can create surprising and beautiful effects in their compositions through the interaction of relative and parallel major and minor keys.

Listen to a recording of the third movement of Chopin's Sonata in B-flat Minor, Op. 35. This composition uses the relative key relationship between B-flat minor and

D-flat major. Chopin begins this movement ("The Funeral March"[1]) in B-flat minor and moves to the relative D-flat major for the middle section of the piece; then he closes in B-flat minor with material from the opening section. The key signature remains the same throughout the movement; the changes between minor and major are achieved by shifting the tonal center (keynote) melodically and harmonically from B-flat to D-flat to B-flat. The main melodic themes are notated in examples 7.1a and 7.1b. Notice that the pitches of the B-flat minor theme move strongly to the last pitch, B-flat (7.1a), and that the pitches of the D-flat major theme move strongly to the last pitch, D-flat (7.1b). This resolution to the melodic pitches B-flat and D-flat, and to the accompanying B-flat minor and D-flat major harmonies, establishes the tonality (key).

7.1a   B-flat minor

7.1b   D-flat major

Listen to the song "Der Lindenbaum" ("The Linden Tree") from Schubert's song cycle *Winterreise.*[2] This is an example of a composition that moves back and forth between a major key and its parallel minor key—in this case, from E major, to E minor, to E major, to E minor, and ending in E major. The main melodic idea is notated as it first appears in E major (example 7.2a) and then as it appears later in E minor (example 7.2b). Notice that the two melodies use the same pitches and resolve to the keynote, E. It is the different key signatures that bring about the changes in mode; they alter the third scale degree of the melody, and the harmony that accompanies this piece.

7.2a   E major

7.2b   E minor

[1,2]A recording of this well-known work should be available in your school or public library.

CONSTRUCTION OF KEY SIGNATURES

Although it is necessary to hear the whole-step or half-step interval between the pitches of a major or a minor scale, there are quicker ways to construct key signatures than working the interval formula to discover the sharped or flatted pitches of the key. Following are two methods of constructing key signatures. The first method is based upon the rules you have already memorized to identify keynotes from written key signatures, and the second method is simply to memorize the Circle of Fifths diagram on page 74.

Writing Major and Minor Key Signatures from a Given Keynote

Sequence of Sharps and Flats in Key Signatures   Both sharps and flats have a specific order of appearance within the various key signatures and a standard placement upon the staff. The first sharp of a sharp key signature is always F, the second is always C, followed by G, D, A, E, and B. The first flat of a flat key signature is always B, the second is always E, followed by A, D, G, C, and F. Sharps and flats never appear together in the same key signature, although sharp accidentals may appear in pieces with a flat key signature and flat accidentals may appear in pieces with a sharp key signature. *Memorize* the following information regarding the sequence of sharps and flats within key signatures and the placement of sharps and flats upon the staff.

Sequence of sharps as they appear in key signature	Each succeeding sharp is five letters above the preceding sharp. Recite the alphabet forward from the first sharp, F.

12345   12345
fgabc   cdefg   etc.
1st ♯   2nd ♯   3rd ♯   4th ♯   5th ♯   6th ♯   7th ♯
F   C   G   D   A   E   B

Sequence of flats as they appear in key signature	Notice that the flat sequence is the reverse of the sharp sequence. Each succeeding flat is five letters below the preceding flat. Recite the alphabet backward from the first flat, B.

12345   12345
bagfe   edcba   etc.
1st ♭   2nd ♭   3rd ♭   4th ♭   5th ♭   6th ♭   7th ♭
B   E   A   D   G   C   F

Placement of seven sharps on the grand staff: Notice the down-up sequence.

Placement of seven flats on the grand staff: Notice the up-down sequence.

Writing Major Key Signatures   To construct major key signatures, *memorize* and use the following procedure.

A. Determine if the key signature you want to write is a flat or a sharp key signature through a process of elimination related to the keynote.

    1. Memorize: The key of C major has no sharps or flats.

    2. Memorize: All major flat key signatures have a flatted keynote except the key of F; F major is the only flat key with a natural keynote.

    3. Memorize: All other major keys, the ones that have natural and sharp keynotes, are sharp keys. Remember that the exceptions are F and C major.

    Examples: The key of B-flat major is a flat key because the keynote is flatted.

                  The key of F-sharp major is a sharp key because the keynote is sharped.

                  The key of B major is a sharp key because the keynote is natural, F major being the only major flat key that has a natural keynote.

B. After you have identified the key signature that you are going to write as a sharp key or a flat key, apply one of the following rules to establish the number and identity of the sharps or flats in the key signature.

    1. Sharp key signatures: The last sharp to the right is the seventh scale degree, one letter (a half step) below the keynote. Write in all the sharps of a key, beginning with F-sharp.

    Example: In the key of B major, A-sharp is the last sharp in the key signature. Write in F-sharp, C-sharp, G-sharp, D-sharp, and A-sharp to construct the key signature.

    2. Flat key signatures: The last flat to the right is the fourth scale degree above the keynote. Write in all the flats of a key, beginning with B-flat. Or beginning with B-flat, write in all the flats to the keynote flat, then add one more flat beyond the keynote. This second rule works with all flat major keys except the key of F major.

    Example: In the key of B-flat major, E-flat is the last flat in the key signature. Write in B-flat and E-flat to construct the key signature.

Write the following major scales using key signatures; then refer to page 66 to see if your key signatures are correct. Sing these scales and perform them on the piano.

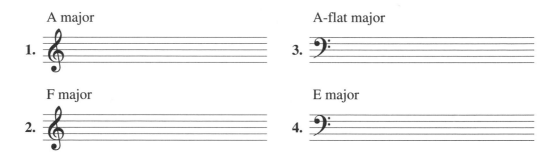

Writing Minor Key Signatures Because key signatures represent both major and minor keys, sharp and flat minor key signatures may be written using the key signatures of their relative major keys. To construct minor key signatures, *memorize* and use the following procedure.

A. Locate the relative major keynote of the minor key signature you want to write. The major keynote is the third scale degree of the minor scale: three letters, one-and-a-half steps, above the minor keynote.

B. Depending upon the major keynote, use either the sharp or the flat key signature rule for writing major key signatures. Write the relative major key signature and you have the relative minor key signature you wanted.

Examples: G-sharp minor has as its relative major the keynote B (three letters, one-and-a-half steps, above G sharp). Construct the key signature for B major; the last sharp to the right is A-sharp. Write in F-sharp, C-sharp, G-sharp, D-sharp, and A-sharp and you have the key signature of G-sharp minor.

G minor has as its relative major the keynote B-flat (three letters, one-and-a-half steps, above G). Construct the key signature for B-flat major; the last flat to the right is E-flat. Write in B-flat and E-flat and you have the key signature of G minor.

Write the following minor scales using key signatures; then refer to page 66 to see if your key signatures are correct. Sing these scales and perform them on the piano.

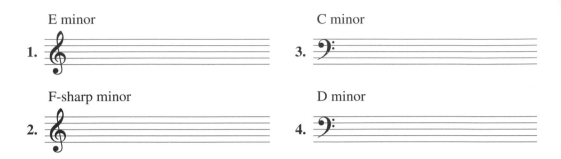

E minor

1.

C minor

3.

F-sharp minor

2.

D minor

4.

The Circle of Fifths

The following diagram is called the **Circle of Fifths**. It includes all the information presented in this chapter regarding key signatures and key relationships. *Memorize* the circle of fifths; it can be used to identify and construct key signatures, identify relative and parallel major and minor keys, and identify the order of sharps (F, up five letters, etc.) and flats (B, down five letters, etc.). It will also be helpful when the subject of chord progressions is presented later in the book.

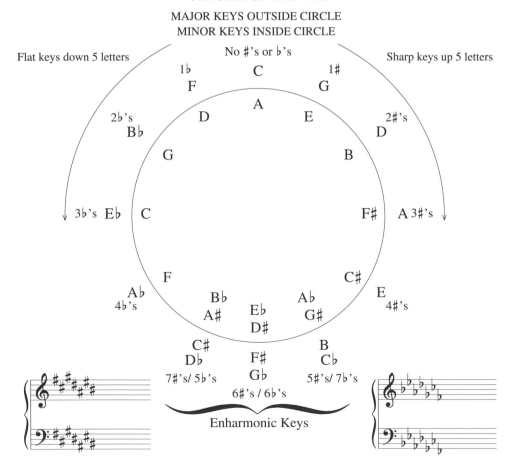

CIRCLE OF FIFTHS

MAJOR KEYS OUTSIDE CIRCLE
MINOR KEYS INSIDE CIRCLE

HARMONIC AND MELODIC MINOR KEYS

Review the information about minor scales presented on pages 53–55 before studying the following information.

The key signature of a harmonic or a melodic minor scale is the same as that of the natural minor scale having the same keynote. The sixth and seventh scale degrees of harmonic and melodic minor scale forms, however, are altered by placing accidentals (sharps, flats, or naturals) before these pitches within the notated scale or music composition. Study the following examples; sing them and perform them on the keyboard.

A. C minor
  1. C natural minor scale

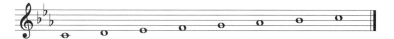

  2. C harmonic minor scale

  3. C melodic minor scale

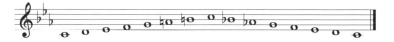

B. D minor
  1. D natural minor scale

  2. D harmonic minor scale

  3. D melodic minor scale

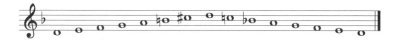

C. E minor

   1. E natural minor scale

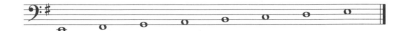

   2. E harmonic minor scale

   3. E melodic minor scale

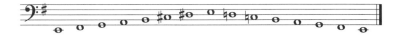

D. Melodic segment in D harmonic minor

E. Melodic segment in C melodic minor

To achieve the proper scale formula for some minor scales, it is necessary to use not only sharps (♯), flats (♭), or naturals (♮) but also **double sharps** (𝄪), which raise the pitch a whole step (e.g., A–double sharp is enharmonic with B-natural). Occasionally you may encounter a **double flat** (♭♭) placed as an accidental within the music you are performing. A double flat lowers a pitch one whole step (e.g., B–double flat is enharmonic with A-natural). Study the following examples; sing them and perform them on the keyboard.

D-sharp harmonic minor scale

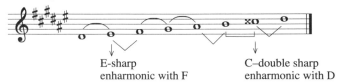

E-sharp
enharmonic with F

C–double sharp
enharmonic with D

G-sharp melodic minor scale

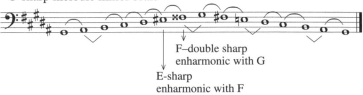

F–double sharp
enharmonic with G

E-sharp
enharmonic with F

Write the following minor scales. Use key signatures, and where necessary, use accidentals to alter the sixth and seventh scale degrees. Refer to page 66 to see if your key signatures are correct. Sing these scales and perform them on the piano.

1. G harmonic minor scale

2. G melodic minor scale

3. B harmonic minor scale

4. B melodic minor scale

IDENTIFYING THE KEY OF A COMPOSITION

Because each key signature represents both the relative major and the relative minor keys, you cannot establish the key of a musical composition by studying the key signature alone. You must also study the pitch content of the piece to establish whether the major keynote or the minor keynote is the pitch that receives special emphasis. This can be done with simple melodies by looking at the last note of the piece, for this pitch is very often the keynote. Keynotes may also occur at the ends of phrases and may appear in the melody more frequently than other scale tones. Furthermore, if the key signature and the ending pitch indicate a minor key, a quick glance through the piece will reveal raised seventh scale degrees for the harmonic minor form, and raised sixth and seventh scale degrees for the melodic minor form.

Study the three melodies notated on pages 78–79. See if you can identify the key of each piece before you consult the key identity given on page 83. After you identify the key, sing each melody using numbers, letters, and words.

EARLY ONE MORNING

Leisurely

England

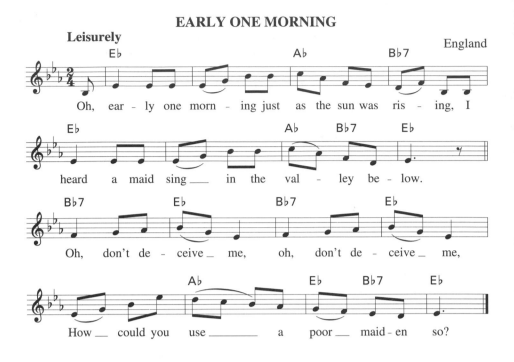

Oh, ear - ly one morn - ing just as the sun was ris - ing, I
heard a maid sing ___ in the val - ley be - low.
Oh, don't de - ceive ___ me, oh, don't de - ceive ___ me,
How ___ could you use ___ a poor ___ maid - en so?

JOSHUA FOUGHT THE BATTLE OF JERICHO

With determination

Spiritual

Josh - ua fought the bat - tle of ___ Jer - i - cho, ___
Jer - i - cho, ___ Jer - i - cho; ___ Josh-ua fought the bat-tle of ___
Jer - i - cho, ___ and the walls came tum - bling down.
You may talk a - bout your kings of Gid - e - on. You may
talk a - bout your men ___ of ___ Saul. But there's none like good old
Josh - ua at the bat - tle of Jer - i - cho.

* **D.C.** is an abbreviation for **da capo,** "from the beginning"; and **al fine** means, "to the end." Both are Italian terms used widely in music notation. This song is sung through line 6 and repeated without pause from the beginning through measure 8, which is marked **Fine,** "end."

GREENSLEEVES

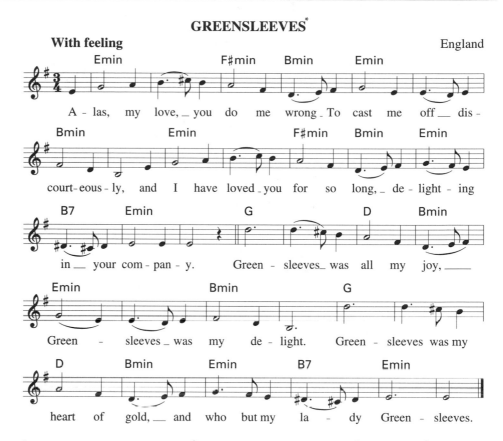

With feeling

England

Emin ... *F#min* ... *Bmin* ... *Emin*

A - las, my love, __ you do me wrong __ To cast me off __ dis -

Bmin ... *Emin* ... *F#min* ... *Bmin* ... *Emin*

court- eous - ly, and I have loved __ you for so long, __ de - light - ing

B7 ... *Emin* ... *G* ... *D* ... *Bmin*

in __ your com - pan - y. Green - sleeves __ was all my joy, _____

Emin ... *Bmin* ... *G*

Green - sleeves __ was my de - light. Green - sleeves was my

D ... *Bmin* ... *Emin* ... *B7* ... *Emin*

heart of gold, __ and who but my la - dy Green - sleeves.

* *Greensleeves* is traditionally notated in ⁶⁄₈ meter. It has been presented here in ³⁄₄ meter because ⁶⁄₈ meter is not introduced until later in the book.

ASSIGNMENT

1. Identify the following key signatures.

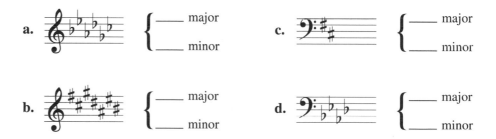

a. {—— major —— minor} **c.** {—— major —— minor}

b. {—— major —— minor} **d.** {—— major —— minor}

2. Write the following scales. Use key signatures, and if pitches within the scale need to be altered, use accidentals. After writing these scales, sing them and play them on a keyboard instrument.

a. B-flat major

b. B major

c. C-sharp natural minor

d. F harmonic minor

e. E-flat major

f. B natural minor

g. The relative melodic minor of B major

h. The relative major of B-flat minor

i. The parallel melodic minor of A major

j. The parallel major of G minor

3. Continue daily performances of rhythm exercises notated in Appendixes A and C. Sing these exercises and play them on a keyboard instrument.

4. Continue improvising rhythm pieces in different meters and various tempos. Sing your improvisations and play them on a keyboard instrument.

5. Continue daily performances of melody exercises notated in Appendix E. Sing these exercises and play them on a keyboard instrument.

6. Use the information from this and previous chapters to improvise melodies based upon different keynotes and different major and minor modes (e.g., A major, B-flat major, E minor, C minor). As you perform, keep the key signature of the scale you are using in your mind. Sing these exercises and play them on a keyboard instrument.

7. Use your knowledge of key signatures to notate and perform your *Original Melody No. 1* (page 49) in the following keys: D major, E-flat major, D minor, and E-flat minor.

Your original melody used the first five pitches of the C major scale, so you will now transpose your piece up one letter to D and use the key signature of D major to notate your first transposed melody.

Next, you will transpose your piece up two letters to E-flat and use the key signature of E-flat major to notate your second melody. These two major melodies will sound just like your melody in C major but at a higher pitch level.

Now change the key signatures of your melodies in D major and E-flat major to their parallel minor keys and notate them in D minor and E-flat minor. The letter names of the pitches will remain the same; the key signature, however, will alter some pitches, so your original major melody will now sound different. Your *Original Melody No. 1* will be a minor melody notated in two different keys.

If while working on these transpositions you feel you can improve your original melody by changing a pitch or rhythm sequence, feel free to do so.

ORIGINAL MELODY NO. 1 IN D MAJOR

ORIGINAL MELODY NO. 1 IN E-FLAT MAJOR

ORIGINAL MELODY NO. 1 IN D MINOR

ORIGINAL MELODY NO. 1 IN E-FLAT MINOR

The keys of the songs presented on pages 78–79 are as follows: *Early One Morning* is in E-flat major; *Joshua Fought the Battle of Jericho* is in D minor (harmonic form); *Greensleeves* begins in E minor (melodic form), moves to the relative key of G major, and ends in E minor.

chapter 8

Hearing and Performing Music in Major and Minor Keys

HEAR THE SCALE, HEAR THE MUSIC

By performing studies in Chapters 3 and 5, you have learned to hear, sing, and play on a keyboard instrument the first five pitches of the C major scale. In this chapter you will learn to hear and perform all the pitches of both the major and the minor scales. First, you will add the sixth and seventh pitches of the C major scale to the five pitches you already know; then you will learn to hear and perform the three primary chords in this key. Next, you will transfer your skills from C major to the C minor mode. Finally, you will learn to use your major and minor performance skills in all keys by transposing the sound of C major and C minor scales to melodies with tonal centers (keys) other than C. Remember, hear the scale, and you will hear the music that was written using the pitches of that particular scale.

Sight Singing

It is important to develop your tonal perception. You must learn to look at a piece of notated music and be able to hear in your mind the exact sound of both the pitches and their rhythmic sequence *before* you perform the music. One of the best ways to develop this skill is to learn to **sight-sing**—to correctly sing notated music upon the first reading without the aid of an accompanying instrument or voice.

There are several methods commonly used to teach sight singing. Two methods will be used throughout this text: the **letter sight-singing method,** which uses the letter names that identify each pitch, the purpose being to develop a sound association with each of the seven letter names; and the **numeral sight-singing method,** which assigns a number to each pitch of the scale, the purpose being to help you memorize the sound of each scale tone and its relationship to other pitches of the scale.

Many vocalists prefer to sing syllables rather than letters or numbers because the sound is more musical. There are two **solfeggio systems** in use. The **fixed-*do* system** uses the following syllables in place of pitch letters: *do* or *doh* for C, *re* for D, *mi* for E, *fa* for F, *sol* for G, *la* for A, and *ti* or *si* for B. This method is similar to the letter system. The **movable-*do* system** uses the same syllables as the fixed-*do* system, but *do* always represents the first scale degree, *re* the second, *mi* the third, and so on. This method is similar to the numerical system. Some people use an elaborate system that changes the syllables for chromatically altered pitches; sharped *do,* for example, may be sung as *dee.*

Memorize the sound of the C major scale, notated in example 8.1, as you play it on the keyboard. Next, sing this scale using the letter method and then the numeral method. Sound only the first pitch of the scale on the piano before you begin to sing.

8.1

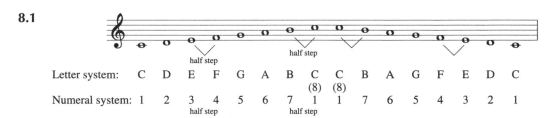

Letter system:	C	D	E	F	G	A	B	C (8)	C (8)	B	A	G	F	E	D	C
Numeral system:	1	2	3	4	5	6	7	1	1	7	6	5	4	3	2	1

The numeral system as an aid to hearing music has two advantages over the letter system. In the letter system, the letter name of the keynote changes each time the key changes; therefore, the entire letter series of the scale is different for each new key. That is not the case with the numeral system. The keynote letter can change for each key, but the first pitch of the scale is always 1, the second pitch is always 2, and so on. Thus, the same interval appears between the same pitch numbers for each scale type, regardless of key, and hearing the scale and its pitch relationships becomes easier. The second advantage of using the numeral system applies to hearing and writing chords that are constructed from scales. In Chapter 10 you will learn that chords are constructed on scale degrees and that they are identified by scale-degree numbers (the chord constructed on the first scale degree is identified as the I chord, the chord constructed on the fourth scale degree is identified as the IV chord, etc.).

Scale/Chord Drills   Scale/chord drills A–E can be applied to all scale types. If practiced seriously, these drills will help you learn to hear scales as a group of pitches that interact melodically and harmonically. These drills are your daily sight-singing vitamin pills. Take a dose everyday in different keys (C, F, G, etc.) and in different modes (major and minor).

Use the numeral system to sing the drills. First, sing while playing the piano. Next, sing without the piano, sounding only the first pitch on the keyboard before you begin to sing. Use the following study sequence.

1. Learn to sing drills A–E in the key of C major. Keep a slow, steady pulse as you give each pitch one beat, and remember that in major scales the half-step intervals are between pitches 3 and 4, and pitches 7 and 1 (8). Once you can sing these drills in major, sing the major melodies in this chapter beginning on page 87.

2. Learn to sing drills A–D in the key of C natural minor. Pitches 3, 6, and 7 will be sung a half step lower than in the parallel C major; these pitch changes place the half steps between pitches 2 and 3, and pitches 5 and 6. For drill E the harmonic minor scale is used, only pitches 3 and 6 are a half step lower than in the parallel major; chords i and iv are minor triads, and the V[7] chord is the same as in the parallel major. Once you can sing these drills in minor, sing the minor melodies in this chapter beginning on page 89.

3. Learn to sing drills A–E in different keys and different modes (e.g., D major, E minor). Once you are comfortable singing these drills in different keys, sing the melodies in different major and minor keys in this chapter beginning on page 91.

A. Scale patterns up and down from the keynote

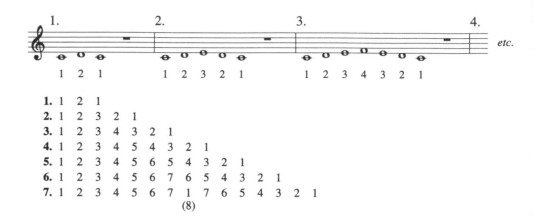

1 2 1   1 2 3 2 1   1 2 3 4 3 2 1   *etc.*

1. 1 2 1
2. 1 2 3 2 1
3. 1 2 3 4 3 2 1
4. 1 2 3 4 5 4 3 2 1
5. 1 2 3 4 5 6 5 4 3 2 1
6. 1 2 3 4 5 6 7 6 5 4 3 2 1
7. 1 2 3 4 5 6 7 1 7 6 5 4 3 2 1
                                (8)

B. Scale patterns down and up from the keynote

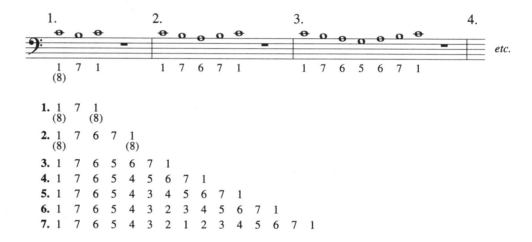

1 7 1   1 7 6 7 1   1 7 6 5 6 7 1   *etc.*
(8)

1. 1 7 1
       (8)   (8)
2. 1 7 6 7 1
       (8)   (8)
3. 1 7 6 5 6 7 1
4. 1 7 6 5 4 5 6 7 1
5. 1 7 6 5 4 3 4 5 6 7 1
6. 1 7 6 5 4 3 2 3 4 5 6 7 1
7. 1 7 6 5 4 3 2 1 2 3 4 5 6 7 1

C. Interval patterns up and down from the keynote to all seven tones of the scale

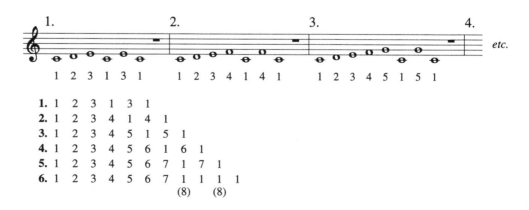

1 2 3 1 3 1   1 2 3 4 1 4 1   1 2 3 4 5 1 5 1   *etc.*

1. 1 2 3 1 3 1
2. 1 2 3 4 1 4 1
3. 1 2 3 4 5 1 5 1
4. 1 2 3 4 5 6 1 6 1
5. 1 2 3 4 5 6 7 1 7 1
6. 1 2 3 4 5 6 7 1 1 1 1
                            (8)   (8)

D. Interval patterns down and up from the keynote to all seven tones of the scale

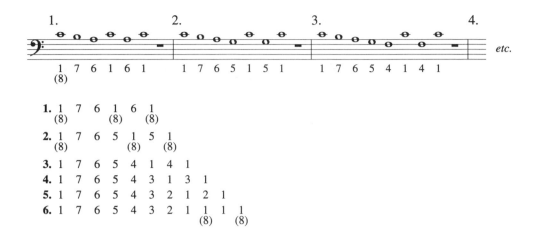

1.	1 (8)	7	6	1 (8)	6	1 (8)			
2.	1 (8)	7	6	5	1 (8)	5	1 (8)		
3.	1	7	6	5	4	1	4	1	
4.	1	7	6	5	4	3	1	3	1
5.	1	7	6	5	4	3	2	1	2	1
6.	1	7	6	5	4	3	2	1	1 (8)	1	1 (8)

THE PRIMARY CHORDS

The three **primary chords** in both major and minor scales are constructed on the first scale degree (**tonic**), the fourth scale degree (**subdominant**), and the fifth scale degree (**dominant**). These three chords include all seven of the scale tones in their construction and are widely used to harmonize melodies in major and minor keys. Chords constructed on other pitches of the scale (2, 3, 6, and 7) will be introduced later and may be considered as substitute harmonies for the primary chords. In drill E the primary chords are presented as **broken chords,** or **arpeggios,** chord tones performed one after the other instead of simultaneously. You will recognize these primary chords as you perform drill E; you learned to hear and sing them when you memorized and performed *Just Sing It!* (examples 1.4 and 1.5).

E. Primary chords in major and harmonic minor

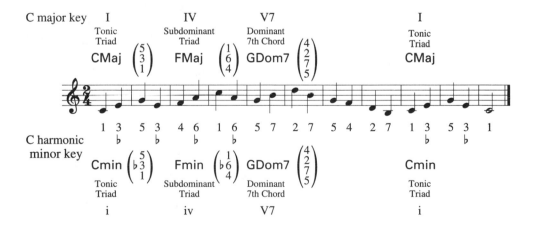

Major Melodies After you have learned to sing the scale/chord drills in C major, sing the following melodies in C major. First, establish the sound of the key in your mind by singing the scale (line 7 of drill A, page 86) and the primary chords (drill E, above) in the key of C major; then sing each melody several times using the numeral sight-singing method; finally, sing each melody using the letter sight-singing method. As you sing, be aware of the way the melodies move by scale tones (diatonically) and by chord tones (skipping).

1. Turn to page 2 and sing *Just Sing It!*

2.

3.

4.

5.

6.

7.

8.

9.

10.

Minor Melodies   After you have learned to sing the scale/chord drills in C minor, sing the following melodies in C minor. These melodies are the same as the preceding major melodies, only presented in the parallel minor mode. First, establish the sound of the key in your mind by singing the scale (line 7 of drill A, page 86) and the primary chords (drill E, page 87) in the key of C minor; then sing each melody several times using the numeral sight-singing method; finally, sing each melody using the letter sight-singing method. As you sing, be aware of the way the melodies move by scale tones (diatonically) and by chord tones (skipping).

In melodies in which the sixth or seventh scale degree is raised (harmonic or melodic minor), these pitches will sound (be performed) like the parallel major sixth or seventh scale degree. Sing only the letter of any pitch that has been flatted, sharped, or made natural, and *hear* the sound lowered or raised by the key signature or an accidental

   1. *Just Sing It!* in C minor (harmonic form)

9.

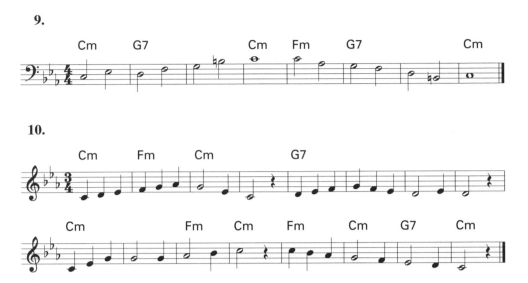

10.

Melodies in Different Major and Minor Keys

Sing the following melodies notated in different major and minor keys. Examine the key signature and the final pitch of each melody to identify its key, then sing and play on the piano the scale (line 7 of drill A, page 86) and the primary chords (drill E, page 87) of the key used to create the melody. After establishing the tonality in your mind, sing each melody using pitch numbers (remember the keynote is always pitch 1); then sing each melody using letters (when pitches are sharped or flatted, sing only the letter and *hear* the sound raised or lowered by the sharp or flat).

1. *Just Sing It!* in B major

2. *Just Sing It!* in A minor

3. B-flat major

*Repeat sign. Repeat music from the beginning without stopping.

4. B-flat minor

5. D major

*Repeat sign. Repeat music between signs without stopping.

6. D minor

7. F major

8. E minor

9. A major

10. G minor

11. E major

12. F-sharp minor

Melodic Dictation in Major and Minor Modes

In Chapter 5 you learned an eight-point procedure for notating dictated melodies (page 42). Use this same procedure to notate recorded melodies 8.2 and 8.3. The scale used to create each melody is written above the exercise. The scale will be played before the melody is dictated; watch the notated scale as it is played, and sing along using pitch numbers. This will help you memorize the scale tones and will make it easier to relate the melody pitches to specific scale tones. Review the procedure on page 42 before beginning.

 8.2 D major scale

Notate the eight-measure melody in D major here.

 8.3 C harmonic minor scale

Notate the eight-measure melody in C minor here.

ASSIGNMENT

1. Identify the major and minor keynotes of the following key signatures.

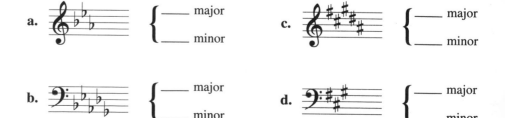

2. Write the following scales. Use key signatures, and if pitches within the scale need to be altered, use accidentals. After writing the scales, sing them and play them on a keyboard instrument.

   a. F major

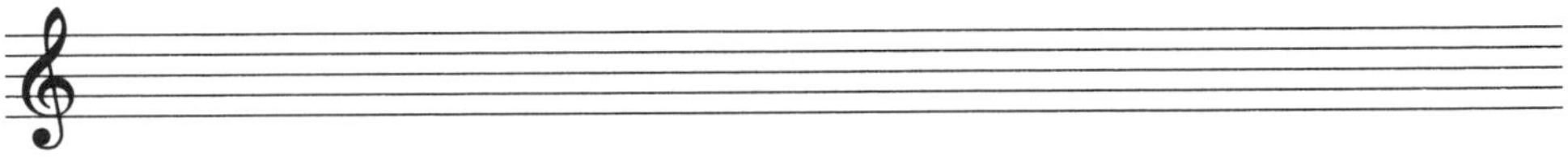

   b. The parallel major of D minor

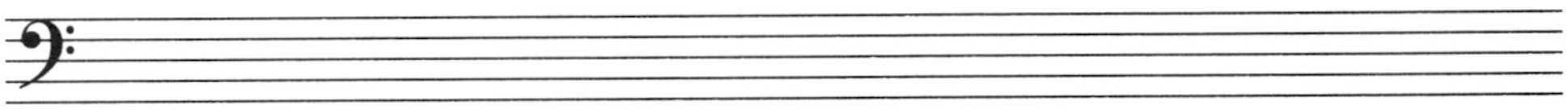

   c. G melodic minor

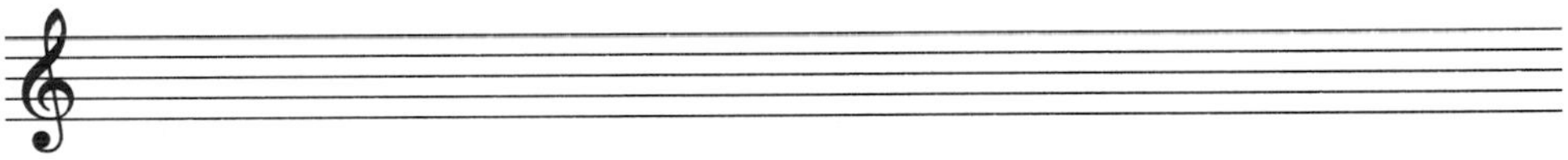

   d. The parallel harmonic minor of E major

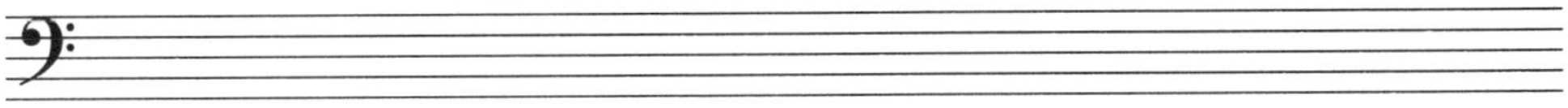

   e. E major

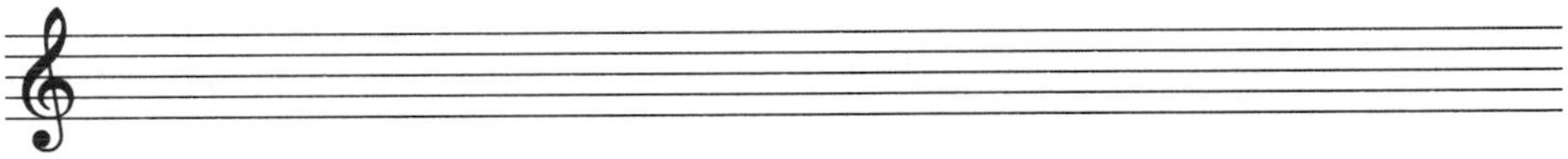

   f. B-flat major

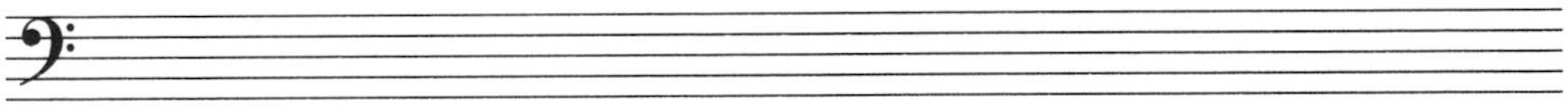

   g. A melodic minor

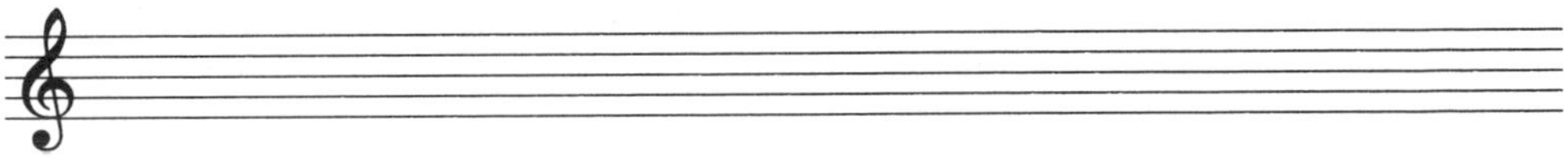

h. The relative natural minor of F-sharp major

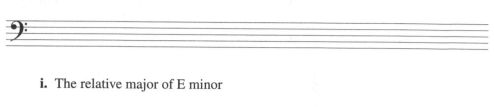

i. The relative major of E minor

j. E-flat harmonic minor

3. Continue daily performances of rhythm exercises notated in Appendixes A and C. Sing these exercises and play them on a keyboard instrument.

4. Continue improvising rhythm pieces in different meters and various tempos.

5. Continue daily performances of scale/chord drills (pages 85–87) in different major and minor keys (C major, D minor, B-flat major, E minor, etc.).

6. Continue daily performances of melody exercises notated in Appendix E, Melodic Studies. Sing without accompaniment. Also perform on a keyboard instrument.

7. Continue improvising melodies in different meters and different keys.

8. Create, notate, and perform a sixteen-measure melody with a four-measure introduction and a four-measure ending (twenty-four measures total). Write your piece in the key of B-flat major or D major. Study and perform *Just Sing It!* (page 2), and think of this song as a model for your original composition. Use the following procedures.

    a. Choose B-flat major or D major for your key; then choose a meter and a tempo that will express the character you have in mind for your melody.

    b. Use all the pitches of the major scale you have chosen, and a variety of rhythms (at least three different note values ♩ ♫ ♩, etc.) to create your piece.

    c. Improvise one phrase at a time; remember to use repeated, sequential, and contrasting musical ideas to give your phrases form. Hear the scale/chord tones in your mind as you improvise, and use scale and chord movement of pitches as you create your melodic ideas.

    d. Choose the best melodic ideas that you have improvised to construct four phrases that work together as two periods (see example 5.42, page 46). This will give your sixteen-measure melody good form. Remember that your melodic ideas should work together to make a musical statement and that the beat is the glue that holds your piece together.

    e. Notate your melody on the staves provided on the next page. Follow the same procedure you used for notating dictated melodies.

    f. Practice performing your melody on the piano, and add appropriate dynamic markings ($\boldsymbol{f}$, $\boldsymbol{p}$, ——, etc.) to make your composition more expressive.

    g. Perform your melody for friends or classmates.

Although there is no such thing as a correct or an incorrect melody, the rhythms and pitches you choose should be properly notated, your manuscript legible, and your performance well prepared.

ORIGINAL MELODY NO. 2 IN MAJOR

chapter **9**

Intervals

MELODIC AND HARMONIC INTERVALS

An **interval** is the distance between two pitches. The classification of an interval serves to identify both the notated (visual) and the sound (aural) relationship that exists between these pitches. When the interval is between two successive tones, it is called a **melodic interval**; when the interval is between two tones sounding simultaneously, it is called a **harmonic interval.** Study, then perform the following examples.

 9.1 Ascending melodic intervals

 9.2 Descending melodic intervals

 9.3 Harmonic intervals

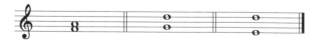

IDENTIFICATION OF NOTATED INTERVALS

Melodic and harmonic intervals are classified by size and by quality. You may identify both of these classifications by relating intervals to the major scale whose tonic is the same as the lower pitch of the interval being identified. Study and *memorize* the following information.

Interval Size

The **size** of an interval is indicated by a numeral that is determined by the number of scale degrees contained within the interval, including the first pitch. In the following example, the lower pitch of each interval is F. In the key of F major there are three scale degrees between the pitches F and A; therefore, both intervals are identified as thirds.

In the next example, the lower pitch of each interval is G. In the key of G major there are four scale degrees between the pitches G and C; therefore, these intervals are identified as fourths.

Study and *memorize* the interval sizes included within a one-octave major scale.

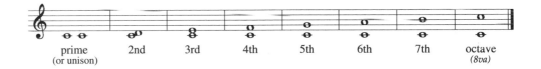

| prime (or unison) | 2nd | 3rd | 4th | 5th | 6th | 7th | octave (*8va*) |

Identify the size of each interval notated below.

1. _____ 2. _____ 3. _____ 4. _____ 5. _____ 6. _____ 7. _____ 8. _____

Interval Quality

The **quality** of an interval is determined by the exact number of half steps contained within the interval. Five interval qualities are encountered in music—**perfect, major, minor, augmented,** and **diminished.** These qualities are most easily identified by relating intervals to the fixed qualities of the intervals formed between the keynote and the other pitches of the major scale. Study and *memorize* the qualities of the eight intervals included in the C major scale notated here. In *all* major scales, primes, fourths, fifths, and octaves are always perfect intervals; seconds, thirds, sixths, and sevenths are always major intervals.

| perfect prime | major 2nd | major 3rd | perfect 4th | perfect 5th | major 6th | major 7th | perfect octave |

To identify the quality of a written interval, think of the major key signature of the lower pitch and then determine the size of the interval. Next, decide if the higher note is a pitch used in the major scale of the lower note; if the higher pitch is a scale tone and it is a second, a third, a sixth, or a seventh, it is a major interval; if it is a prime, a fourth, a fifth, or an octave, it is a perfect interval. In the following example, the lower pitch is F; think of the key of F major with one flat (B-flat). The pitch A is the third scale tone above F major; the interval is therefore a major third.

Interval of a major 3rd

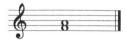

In the next example, the lower pitch is E-flat; think of the key of E-flat major with three flats (B-flat, E-flat, and A-flat). The pitch B-flat is the fifth scale tone above E-flat major; the interval is therefore a perfect fifth.

Interval of a perfect 5th

Identify the quality and the size of the intervals written below. All intervals should be related to the key of G major.

Quality: 1. _____ 2. _____ 3. _____ 4. _____ 5. _____ 6. _____ 7. _____ 8. _____

Size: _____   _____   _____   _____   _____   _____   _____   _____

Identify the intervals written below. Each interval must be related to a different key.

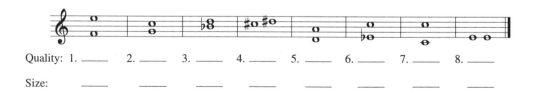

Quality: 1. _____ 2. _____ 3. _____ 4. _____ 5. _____ 6. _____ 7. _____ 8. _____

Size: _____   _____   _____   _____   _____   _____   _____   _____

Although primes, fourths, fifths, and octaves above the keynote of a major scale are *always perfect,* and seconds, thirds, sixths, and sevenths above the keynote of a major scale are *always major,* the qualities of these intervals may be changed by expanding or contracting the intervals. Study and *memorize* the following information.

1. A major interval expanded a half step becomes an augmented interval.

2. A major interval contracted a half step becomes a minor interval.

3. A major interval contracted two half steps (one whole step) becomes a diminished interval.

4. A perfect interval expanded a half step becomes an augmented interval.

5. A perfect interval contracted a half step becomes a diminished interval.

Although major intervals (seconds, thirds, sixths, and sevenths) may be expanded or contracted to form augmented, minor, and diminished intervals, they are *never* classified as perfect. Likewise, perfect intervals (primes, fourths, fifths, and octaves) may be expanded or contracted to form augmented and diminished intervals, but they are *never* classified as major or minor.

COMPOUND INTERVALS

The intervals you have studied so far—an octave or smaller—are called **simple intervals.** Intervals larger than an octave are called **compound intervals.** The first five compound intervals also have special names: **ninth, tenth, eleventh, twelfth,** and **thirteenth.** The quality of a compound interval is the same as its simple interval located an octave below. For example, a ninth's simple interval is a second (9 less the 7 letters within an octave equals 2); ninths, therefore, will have the same qualities as seconds (9 − 7 = 2), tenths the same qualities as thirds (10 − 7 = 3), and so forth. Study and *memorize* the following compound intervals.

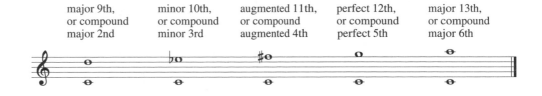

Study and *memorize* Table 3. It will help you see at a glance how intervals may be identified by relating them to the fixed major and perfect qualities that exist between the keynote and the other pitches of the major scale.

TABLE 3   Intervals

Intervals of a 2nd, 3rd, 6th, or 7th are	**Augmented**	if higher pitch is one half step higher than the pitch required to form a major interval.
	Major	if higher pitch is in the major scale of the lower pitch.
	Minor	if higher pitch is one half step lower than the pitch required to form a major interval.
	Diminished	if higher pitch is one half step lower than the pitch required to form a minor interval (or a whole step lower than the pitch required to form a major interval).
Intervals of a prime, 4th, 5th, or octave are	**Augmented**	if higher pitch is one half step higher than the pitch required to form a perfect interval.
	Perfect	if higher pitch is in the major scale of the lower pitch.
	Diminished	if higher pitch is one half step lower than the pitch required to form a perfect interval.

Identify the following intervals.

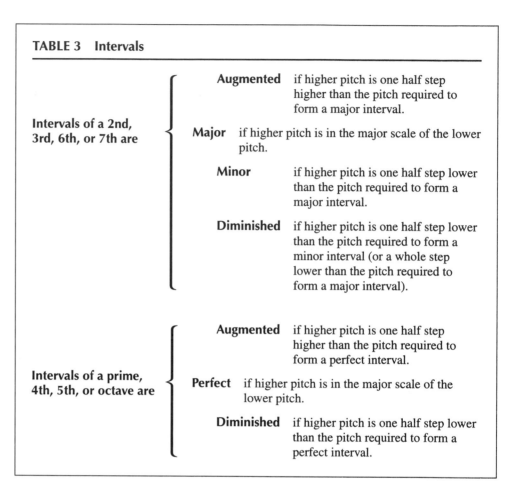

Quality: 1. _____   2. _____   3. _____   4. _____   5. _____

Size: _____   _____   _____   _____   _____

Write the following intervals by placing the correct pitches above the given notes.

maj. 6th   maj. 3rd   min. 7th   aug. prime   perf. 11th

INVERTED INTERVALS

An interval may be **inverted** by placing the higher pitch an octave lower or by placing the lower pitch an octave higher. For example, the interval between the pitches G and D may appear in the following inversions.

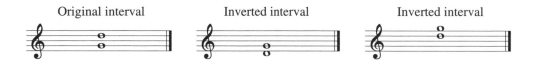

Original interval   Inverted interval   Inverted interval

When an interval is inverted its size is changed, and the size of the original interval plus the size of the inverted interval always totals 9; for example an inverted fourth becomes a fifth (4 + 5 = 9). Study and *memorize* the following information.

Primes (1) inverted become octaves (8).   Seconds inverted become sevenths.

Thirds inverted become sixths.   Fourths inverted become fifths.

Fifths inverted become fourths.   Sixths inverted become thirds.

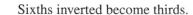

Sevenths inverted become seconds.   Octaves inverted become primes.

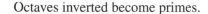
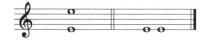

When a major, a minor, an augmented, or a diminished interval is inverted, its quality is also changed. Study and *memorize* the following information.

All major intervals inverted become minor.   All minor intervals inverted become major.

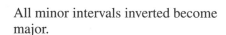

    maj. 3rd   min. 6th   min. 2nd   maj. 7th

All diminished intervals inverted become augmented.

All augmented intervals inverted become diminished.

Although perfect intervals change size when they are inverted, their quality remains the same; hence their name, perfect.

Identify the following intervals; then notate the inversion of each interval in the blank measure and identify it.

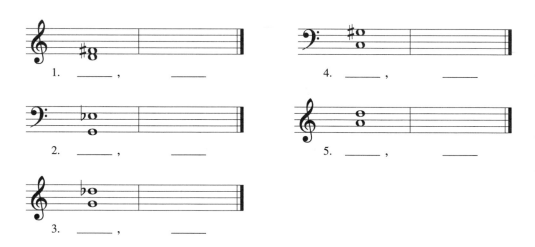

1. _____ , _____

2. _____ , _____

3. _____ , _____

4. _____ , _____

5. _____ , _____

AURAL IDENTIFICATION OF MELODIC INTERVALS— TWO METHODS

It is important that you learn to recognize the sounds of melodic intervals. Having this skill will improve your ability to hear notated music you wish to perform. It will also make it possible for you to notate melodies that you hear others perform or compositions that you create.

Method One

If you can sing one or two songs from memory, you have already memorized the sounds of many melodic intervals, for singing familiar melodies is nothing more than memorizing the sounds and sequential order of intervals and rhythms used in a given piece of music. That being the case, you now need only give the proper name to the sounds you have already memorized and learn the sound and name of any interval you may not recognize.

For example, if you are able to sing the first two notes of *The Star-Spangled Banner,* then you already know what the descending interval of a minor third sounds like.

9.4

If you can sing *Are You Sleeping? (Frère Jacques)*, then you have already memorized the sound of an ascending major second.

9.5

You already know the sound of an ascending perfect fourth if you can sing the opening to *Auld Lang Syne.*

9.6

You can learn to identify both ascending and descending intervals by associating their sounds with the opening pitches of familiar songs. See Table 4 (pages 108–109, the columns under "Interval/Song Association") for songs that can be used to identify melodic intervals. If some of these songs are not familiar to you, then play the interval you want to learn on a keyboard instrument and ask yourself, "What song do I know that begins with this sound?" When you have thought of a song, use it for your interval/song association.

Method Two

You may also identify the sound of an interval by associating it with the major scale, the same way you identify notated intervals (see Table 3, page 102). Think of the lower sounding pitch as the keynote of a major scale and sing up the scale to the higher sounding pitch to determine the interval's size and quality. Study and perform the following examples of this method of interval identification (9.7 and 9.8); then study Table 4, pages 108–109, the column subtitled "Interval from Keynote."

9.7

9.8

Interval

In the key of G major,
B-flat is a half step lower
than the third scale degree.
This interval is a *minor* 3rd.

TWELVE BASIC INTERVAL SOUNDS

Because there are only twelve pitches within an octave, there are only twelve basic interval sounds (see Table 4, pages 108–109). All twelve of these intervals can be heard between the various pitches of the major scale, and some intervals—such as the major second—can be heard between many different scale degrees. These twelve intervals include many perfect, major, and minor intervals, but *only one of the twelve sounds represents an augmented or a diminished interval.*

Both the augmented fourth and the diminished fifth may be notated between the fourth and seventh scale degrees of a major scale. Although these two intervals look different, *they sound identical,* so they cannot be distinguished by sound. Therefore, the name **tritone** (three whole steps) is given to the augmented fourth and diminished fifth sound. When you hear this unique sound, you should identify it as a tritone. When you see one of these intervals written, you should identify it as either an augmented fourth or a diminished fifth. *Memorize:* You hear only one augmented or diminished sound; it is the tritone. See the following examples.

The augmented 4th has the same tritone sound as the diminished 5th.

Other augmented and diminished intervals (aug. 3rd, dim. 6th, etc.) are enharmonic notations of major, minor, or perfect intervals, and they are identified when heard as major, minor, or perfect sounds. For example, a diminished third sounds like a major second, and you should identify it as a major second when you hear it; an augmented third sounds like a perfect fourth, and you should identify it as a perfect fourth when you hear it. See the following examples.

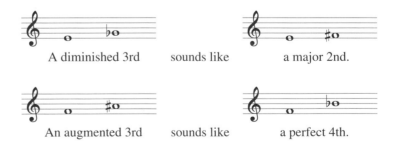

A diminished 3rd   sounds like   a major 2nd.

An augmented 3rd   sounds like   a perfect 4th.

Because the augmented and diminished intervals—other than the augmented fourth and the diminished fifth—are enharmonic spellings of major, minor, or perfect intervals, *the numerous written intervals encountered in music can be reduced to only **twelve basic interval sounds.*** You must memorize the sounds of these twelve intervals.

Study Table 4 (pages 108–109), and *memorize* the information that you feel is most helpful in your effort to learn the twelve basic interval sounds. Then play each of the twelve intervals up and down on the keyboard, and sing them over and over until you have memorized the unique sound of each interval.

Aural Melodic Interval Drills   Use the following recorded exercises as drills to further develop your ability to sing or recognize the sound of melodic intervals. Study these exercises until you can sing and identify the twelve basic melodic interval sounds quickly and correctly. For additional training in this area, create and record your own drills similar to exercises 9.10–9.12, but use different pitches and interval sequences.

9.10   The intervals notated here will be played on recording 9.10 so that you can sing and memorize these interval sounds. After you have heard the name and the sound of the interval, pause the recording so that you can sing and memorize the interval sound.

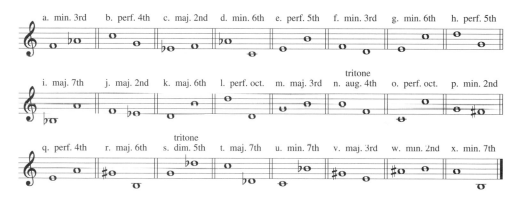

9.11   On recording 9.11 you will hear a melodic interval performed. After you have heard the interval, pause the recording so that you can identify it. Next, release the pause and the interval will be played again and named so that you can check your identification. Twenty-four intervals will be performed; they are also identified in Appendix H.

9.12   Sing the intervals notated here. On recording 9.12 you will hear the name of each interval you are to sing and only the first pitch of the interval. After you have heard this information, pause the recording so that you can sing the two pitches that make up the interval. Next, release the pause and both pitches of the interval will be performed so that you can check the pitches you sang.

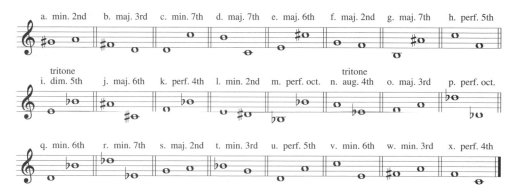

9.9

TABLE 4   The Twelve Basic Interval Sounds Related to Major Scale Degrees and Songs

Interval	Interval from Keynote	Interval within Scale (Up and Down)	Melody Up	Melody Down
	Interval/Major Scale Association		**Interval/Song Association**	
Minor 2nd	1–♭2	7–1 or 1–7 3–4 or 4–3	**As Time Goes By** "You must remember . . ." 3, 4	**Joy to the World** 1, 7
			Pink Panther Theme Raised 6, lowered 7 (melodic minor)	**Joshua Fought the Battle of Jericho** 1, 7 (harmonic minor)
Major 2nd	1–2	1–2 or 2–1 2–3 or 3–2 4–5 or 5–4 5–6 or 6–5 6–7 or 7–6	**Are You Sleeping?** 1, 2	**Three Blind Mice** 3, 2

Minor 3rd	1–♭3	2–4 or 4–2
		3–5 or 5–3
		6–1 or 1–6
		7–2 or 2–7
			Greensleeves
			"Alas my love . . ."
			  1,3 (melodic minor)
				The Star-Spangled Banner
				"Oh,–say, can . . ."
				  5,3

Major 3rd	1–3	1–3 or 3–1 4–6 or 6–4 5–7 or 7–5	**The Marines' Hymn** "From the halls . . ." 1, 3	**Swing Low, Sweet Chariot** 3, 1
Perfect 4th	1–4	1–4 or 4–1 2–5 or 5–2 3–6 or 6–3 5–1 or 1–5 6–2 or 2–6 7–3 or 3–7	**Auld Land Syne** "Should auld . . ." 5, 1	**When Johnny Comes Marching** 1, 5 **Home** (minor)
Tritone (Aug. 4th or Dim. 5th)	1–♯4 or 1–♭5	4–7 or 7–4 7–4 or 4–7	**Maria** (*West Side Story*) 1, ♯4	
Perfect 5th	1–5	1–5 or 5–1 2–6 or 6–2 3–7 or 7–3 4–1 or 1–4 5–2 or 2–5 6–3 or 3–6	**Twinkle, Twinkle, Little Star** 1, (1), 5	**The Star-Spangled Banner** "Oh, –say, . . ." 5, (3), 1 **Feelings** 5, 1 (minor)

Minor 6th	1–♭6	3–1 or 1–3
		6–4 or 4–6
		7–5 or 5–7
			Go Down, Moses
			"When Israel was . . ."
			  5, 3 (minor)
				Theme from *Love Story*
				"Where do I . . ."
				  3, 5 (minor)

Major 6th	1–6	1–6 or 6–1 2–7 or 7–2 4–2 or 2–4 5–3 or 3–5	**NBC** (Network, ID tones) 5,3	**Nobody Knows the Trouble I've** 3, 5 **Seen**

TABLE 4 (continued)

Interval	Interval from Keynote	Interval within Scale (Up and Down)	Melody Up	Melody Down
	Interval/Major Scale Association		Interval/Song Association	
Minor 7th	1–♭7	2–1 or 1–2 3–2 or 2–3 5–4 or 4–5 6–5 or 5–6 7–6 or 6–7	**Somewhere** (*West Side Story*) "There's a place . . ." 5, 4	**White Christmas** (end) ". . .Christmases be white" 6, 7, (7, 7, 1)
Major 7th	1–7	1–7 or 7–1 4–3 or 3–4	**Bali Hai** (*South Pacific*) 5,(5)♯4	**I Love You** 5,(5), ♭6
Perfect Octave	1–8	1–8 or 8–1 (1) (1) 2–2 or 2–2 3–3 or 3–3 *etc. etc.*	**Over the Rainbow** "Somewhere . . ." 1, 8	**Willow Weep For Me** 5, 5

IDENTIFYING HARMONIC INTERVALS BY SOUND—TWO METHODS

Because most of the music you listen to and perform includes harmonic sounds, it is important that you develop the ability to recognize the sounds of the various harmonic intervals. As with melodic intervals, there are numerous written harmonic intervals but only twelve different harmonic interval sounds within one octave.

Method One

When you hear two pitches performed simultaneously, you may identify the resulting harmonic interval by separating the pitches in your mind and thinking of them as a melodic interval; then you will be able to recognize the harmonic sound using the same technique you have developed for identifying melodic intervals (scale degrees or song association). Be careful, however, not to invert the interval when you separate the pitches, for inverting the interval will change its classification.

9.13   Hear the harmonic interval;   think of the melodic interval.

maj. 3rd

maj. 3rd

9.14   Hear the harmonic interval;   think of the melodic interval.

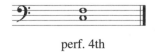

perf. 4th

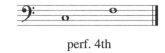

perf. 4th

9.15 Hear the harmonic interval;   think of the melodic interval.

   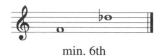

min. 6th   min. 6th

Method Two

The second method of identifying harmonic intervals involves a three-step procedure that is related to the interval's size, quality, and consonant or dissonant characteristic. A harmonic interval is considered **consonant** if the sound it produces is restful, or agreeable. It is considered **dissonant** if the resulting harmonic sound is restless, or harsh. Listen to, study, and *memorize* recorded example 9.16 (Table 5).

          9.16

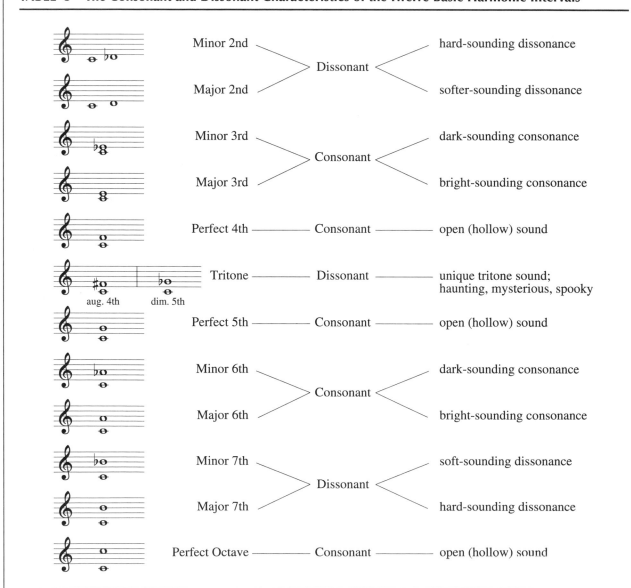

TABLE 5	The Consonant and Dissonant Characteristics of the Twelve Basic Harmonic Intervals

Interval	Consonant/Dissonant	Characteristic
Minor 2nd	Dissonant	hard-sounding dissonance
Major 2nd	Dissonant	softer-sounding dissonance
Minor 3rd	Consonant	dark-sounding consonance
Major 3rd	Consonant	bright-sounding consonance
Perfect 4th	Consonant	open (hollow) sound
Tritone (aug. 4th / dim. 5th)	Dissonant	unique tritone sound; haunting, mysterious, spooky
Perfect 5th	Consonant	open (hollow) sound
Minor 6th	Consonant	dark-sounding consonance
Major 6th	Consonant	bright-sounding consonance
Minor 7th	Dissonant	soft-sounding dissonance
Major 7th	Dissonant	hard-sounding dissonance
Perfect Octave	Consonant	open (hollow) sound

Compound harmonic intervals have the same consonant or dissonant characteristic as their simple intervals. For example, a major ninth is dissonant like its simple interval, the major second; the minor tenth is consonant like its simple interval, the minor third.

Now that you are familiar with the consonant and dissonant characteristics of the twelve basic harmonic intervals, you are ready to apply the following three-step procedure for identifying harmonic intervals. This procedure uses a process of elimination that leads to the correct interval identification. At first, the process may seem slow and laborious; but with practice you will be able to apply all three steps in an instant, as if they were really a one-step process. Try it! It is much faster and safer than identifying harmonic intervals as if they were melodic intervals. Study, *memorize,* and use the following procedure.

**THREE-STEP PROCEDURE FOR IDENTIFYING
HARMONIC INTERVALS**

1. Decide if the interval you hear is consonant or dissonant as described in Table 5 on page 110. Then apply steps 2 and 3 for dissonant or for consonant intervals.

Dissonant Intervals

2. Determine the size of the dissonant interval. Ask yourself if the interval sounds *close* like a second, *wide* like a seventh, or exactly one-half an octave like the unique tritone.

3. Identify the specific interval by determining the exact nature of its dissonance. If it is not a close or a wide interval, it is the unique-sounding tritone. If the interval is the close sound of a second, ask yourself if it is the hard (biting) dissonance of the minor second or the softer (less biting) dissonance of the major second. If the interval is the wide sound of a seventh, ask yourself if it is the hard (biting) dissonance of the major seventh or the softer (less biting) dissonance of the minor seventh.

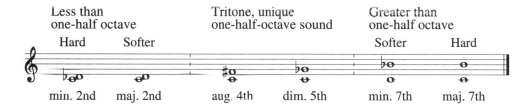

Less than one-half octave		Tritone, unique one-half-octave sound		Greater than one-half octave	
Hard	Softer			Softer	Hard
min. 2nd	maj. 2nd	aug. 4th	dim. 5th	min. 7th	maj. 7th

Consonant Intervals

2. Determine the size of the consonant interval. Ask yourself if the interval sounds less than or greater than one-half an octave, the unique tritone sound. If it is less, it will be a third or a fourth; if it is greater, it will be a fifth, a sixth, or an octave.

3. Identify the specific interval by determining the exact nature of its consonance. Ask yourself if the interval has the open (hollow) sound of a perfect interval (narrow perfect fourth, wider perfect fifth, widest perfect octave), the bright sound of a major interval (narrow major third, wide major sixth), or the dark sound of a minor interval (narrow minor third, wide minor sixth).

Less than one-half octave			Greater than one-half octave			
Dark	Bright	Open	Open	Dark	Bright	Open
min. 3rd	maj. 3rd	perf. 4th	perf. 5th	min. 6th	maj. 6th	perf. oct.

Aural Harmonic Interval Drills

Use the following recorded exercises as drills to further develop your ability to recognize the sound of harmonic intervals. Study these exercises until you can identify the twelve basic harmonic interval sounds quickly and correctly. For additional training in this area, create and record your own drills similar to exercises 9.17–9.19, but use different pitches and interval sequences.

9.17 The intervals notated here will be played on recording 9.17 so that you can sing and memorize these interval sounds. After you have heard the name and the sound of the interval, pause the recording so that you can practice separating the pitches in your mind and sing the harmonic interval as a melodic interval—lower pitch to higher pitch and vice versa.

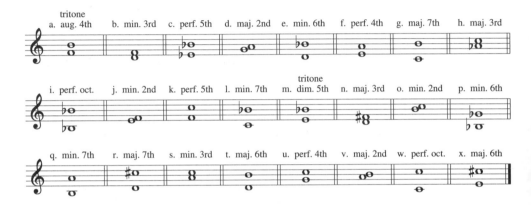

9.18 On recording 9.18 you will hear a harmonic interval performed. After you have heard the interval, pause the recording so that you can identify the interval. Next, release the pause and the interval will be played again and named so that you can check your identification. Twenty-four intervals will be performed; they are also identified in Appendix H.

9.19 Sing the harmonic intervals notated here. On recording 9.19 you will hear the name of each interval you are to sing. Then the tied half notes will be performed and held while you sing the accompanying half note to produce the harmonic sound asked for. Next, both pitches of the harmonic interval will be performed so that you can check the pitch you sang.

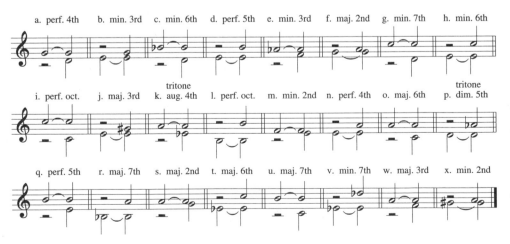

ASSIGNMENT

1. Circle the harmonic intervals that are consonant.

   Maj. 7th   Perf. 5th   Min. 3rd   Aug. 4th   Maj. 3rd   Maj. 2nd

   Perf. 4th   Min. 6th   Min. 2nd   Perf. Oct.   Maj. 6th

2. Circle the harmonic intervals that are dissonant.

   Perf. 4th   Maj. 2nd   Dim. 5th   Maj. 6th   Min. 3rd   Aug. 4th

   Maj. 3rd   Min. 2nd   Min. 7th   Perf. 5th   Maj. 7th

3. Write the following scales. Use key signatures, and if pitches within the scales need to be altered, use accidentals. After writing each scale, play it on the piano, then sing it using numbers and letters.

   a. F-sharp melodic minor

   b. B major

   c. The relative harmonic minor of D-flat major

   d. The parallel natural minor of E major

4. Identify the key of each piece notated below. Then sing each melody, first using pitch numbers, then using letters.

   a. Key of _____

   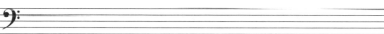

   b. Key of _____

   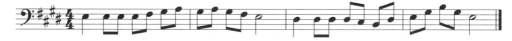

5. Identify the following intervals; then notate the inversion of each interval in the blank measure and identify it.

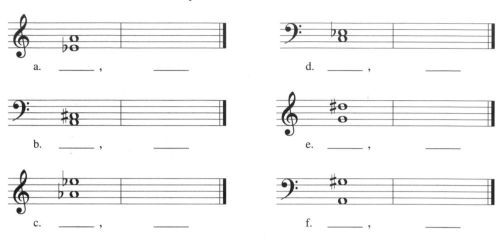

a. _____ , _____   d. _____ , _____

b. _____ , _____   e. _____ , _____

c. _____ , _____   f. _____ , _____

6. Write the following intervals by placing the correct pitches *above* the given notes.

maj. 7th   perf. 5th   min. 3rd   maj. 6th   dim. 5th

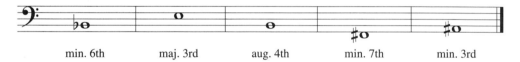

min. 6th   maj. 3rd   aug. 4th   min. 7th   min. 3rd

7. Write the following intervals by placing the correct pitches *below* the given notes. (By thinking of the inversion of the interval asked for, you can think in the major key of the given note and find the correct pitch quickly.)

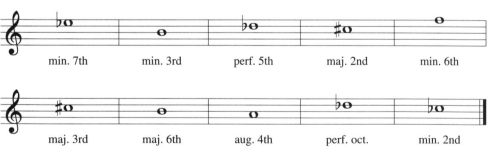

min. 7th   min. 3rd   perf. 5th   maj. 2nd   min. 6th

maj. 3rd   maj. 6th   aug. 4th   perf. oct.   min. 2nd

8. Identify the melodic and harmonic intervals performed on recordings 9.20a and 9.20b or by your instructor. These intervals are identified in Appendix H.

9.20a   Melodic intervals

(1) _____   (4) _____   (7) _____   (10) _____

(2) _____   (5) _____   (8) _____   (11) _____

(3) _____   (6) _____   (9) _____   (12) _____

9.20b   Harmonic intervals

(1) _____   (4) _____   (7) _____   (10) _____

(2) _____   (5) _____   (8) _____   (11) _____

(3) _____   (6) _____   (9) _____   (12) _____

9. Create, notate, and perform a sixteen-measure melody with a four-measure introduction and a four-measure ending (twenty-four measures total). Write your piece in the key of D minor or E minor. Study and perform *Just Sing It!* (page 89), and think of this song as a model for your original composition. Use the following procedures.

   a. Choose D minor or E minor for your key; then choose a meter and a tempo that will express the character you have in mind for your melody.

   b. Use all the pitches of the minor scale you have chosen, and a variety of rhythms (at least three different note values ♩ ♫ ♩, etc.) to create your piece.

   c. Improvise one phrase at a time; remember to use repeated, sequential, and contrasting musical ideas to give your phrases form. Hear the scale/chord tones in your mind as you improvise, and use scale and chord movement of pitches as you create your melodic ideas.

   d. Choose the best melodic ideas that you have improvised to construct four phrases that work together as two periods (see example 5.42, page 46). This will give your sixteen-measure melody good form. Remember that your melodic ideas should work together to make a musical statement and that the beat is the glue that holds your piece together.

   e. Notate your melody on the staff provided below. Follow the same procedure you used for notating dictated melodies.

   f. Practice performing your melody on the piano, and add appropriate dynamic markings (*f*, *p*, ——, etc.) to make your composition more expressive.

   g. Perform your melody for friends or classmates.

   Although there is no such thing as a correct or an incorrect melody, the rhythms and pitches you choose should be properly notated, your manuscript legible, and your performance well prepared.

ORIGINAL MELODY NO. 3 IN MINOR

chapter *10*

Triads and Seventh Chords

CHORD STRUCTURE

Harmonic sounds are basic to most styles of music, and when several pitches, usually three or more, are performed at the same time, the resulting harmonic sound is called a **chord.** Although a chord may be constructed using various intervals or combinations of intervals between its pitches, those constructed with major and minor thirds between chord tones are most widely used. This chapter presents information that all musicians need to know about how chords are constructed, how they relate to the major/minor tonal system, and how they can be used to harmonize melodies. Study and perform the following examples.

10.1 Chords constructed from major and minor thirds (**tertian** harmony)

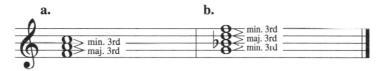

10.2 Chords constructed from perfect fourths (**quartal** harmony)

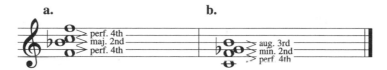

10.3 Chords constructed from a combination of intervals

TRIAD STRUCTURE

A chord consisting of three tones, the adjacent pitches being a third apart, is called a **triad.** Triads are the basic chords of tonal harmony, and they are classified by a letter name and a quality. The **letter name** of the triad is the same as the **root** of the triad, the lowest of the three pitches that make up the triad. The **quality** of a triad is determined by the intervals that exist between the root and the chord tones a third and a fifth above the root. There are only four **quality classifications of triads: major, minor, diminished,** and **augmented.**

Study and *memorize* the intervallic structure of major, minor, diminished, and augmented triads, illustrated in the following four examples. Play these triads.

Major triads (root, major 3rd, perfect 5th)

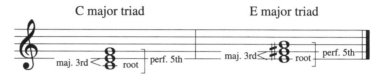

Minor triads (root, minor 3rd, perfect 5th)

Diminished triads (root, minor 3rd, diminished 5th)

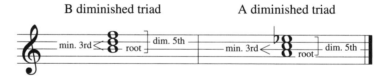

Augmented triads (root, major 3rd, augmented 5th)

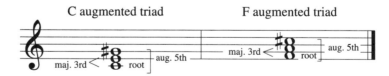

Write the following major triads by notating a major third and a perfect fifth above the given roots. Play these triads.

Write the following minor triads by notating a minor third and a perfect fifth above the given roots. Play these triads.

Write the following diminished triads by notating a minor third and a diminished fifth above the given roots. Play these triads.

Write the following augmented triads by notating a major third and an augmented fifth above the given roots. Play these triads.

Identify these triads (B-flat maj., A min., F-sharp dim., D aug., etc.).

IDENTIFYING TRIADS BY SOUND—TWO METHODS

Because triads are present in much of the music you listen to and perform, it is important that you learn to recognize them by sound as well as by sight. This task is somewhat easier than identifying melodic and harmonic intervals because there are only four different triads to recognize—major, minor, diminished, and augmented—each with its own distinctive sound. Following are two methods of identifying triads by sound.

Method One

When you hear a triad performed, you can separate the pitches in your mind and think of the three pitches as an arpeggio (a broken chord). The arpeggio can then be heard and identified as two melodic intervals: a third between the root and the third of the triad, and a fifth between the root and the fifth of the triad; or as a third between the root and the third of the triad, and a third between the third and the fifth of the triad. Study, perform, and memorize the sounds of the following examples.

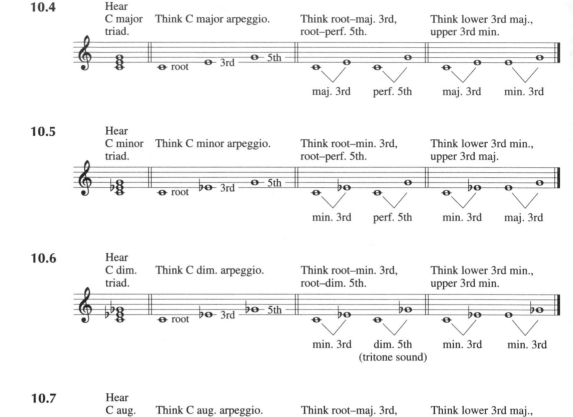

To further develop your ability to hear triads, practice performing the following triad exercises. Play a C major triad on the piano as you sing the following C major triad arpeggio figures. Also perform this drill as C minor, C diminished, and C augmented triads.

Piano Fingering: R.H. (root) 1, (3rd) 3, (5th) 5
L.H. (root) 5, (3rd) 3, (5th) 1

Method Two

Triads, like harmonic intervals, may be identified by their consonant or dissonant characteristics and by the application of a two-step procedure. Listen to, study, and *memorize* the following recorded examples of Table 6.

10.8

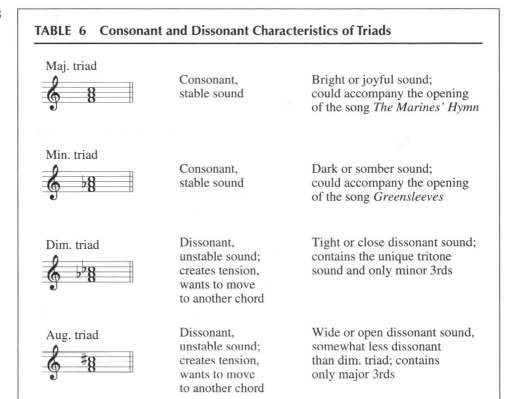

TABLE 6 Consonant and Dissonant Characteristics of Triads

Maj. triad	Consonant, stable sound	Bright or joyful sound; could accompany the opening of the song *The Marines' Hymn*
Min. triad	Consonant, stable sound	Dark or somber sound; could accompany the opening of the song *Greensleeves*
Dim. triad	Dissonant, unstable sound; creates tension, wants to move to another chord	Tight or close dissonant sound; contains the unique tritone sound and only minor 3rds
Aug. triad	Dissonant, unstable sound; creates tension, wants to move to another chord	Wide or open dissonant sound, somewhat less dissonant than dim. triad; contains only major 3rds

Now that you are familiar with the consonant and dissonant characteristics of the four triads, you are ready to apply the following two-step procedure for identifying triads. This procedure uses a process of elimination that leads to the correct triad identification. You will find that this method is quicker than Method One. Study, *memorize,* and use the following procedure.

TWO-STEP PROCEDURE FOR IDENTIFYING TRIADS

1. Listen carefully to the sound of the triad and decide if it is consonant (stable sound without tension) or dissonant (unstable sound that creates tension). Then apply step 2 for consonant or for dissonant triads.

Consonant Triad

2. If the triad is consonant, identify it by determining the exact nature of its consonance. Ask yourself if the triad has the bright, joyful sound of a major triad or the dark, somber sound of a minor triad.

Dissonant Triad

2. If the triad is dissonant, identify it by determining the exact nature of its dissonance. Ask yourself if the triad has the tight, close, unique tritone sound of the diminished triad or the wide, open, and less dissonant sound of the augmented triad.

Aural Triad Drills   Use the following recorded exercises as drills to further develop your ability to recognize the sounds of triads. Study these exercises until you can identify the four types of triad sounds quickly and correctly. For additional training in this area, create and record your own drills similar to exercises 10.9–10.15; use triads built upon different pitches (roots) and play them in different major, minor, diminished, and augmented sequences.

    10.9   The triads notated here will be played on recording 10.9 so that you can memorize the consonant and dissonant characteristics of major, minor, diminished, and augmented triads. After you have heard the sound of each triad and its consonant or dissonant characteristic has been identified, pause the recording so you can assimilate the sound and its consonant or dissonant classification.

    10.10   On recording 10.10 you will hear a major, a minor, a diminished, or an augmented triad performed. After you have heard the triad, pause the recording so that you can identify it as consonant or dissonant. Next, release the pause and the triad will be played again and its consonant or dissonant characteristic identified so that you can check your answer. Twelve triads will be played; they are also identified in Appendix H.

    10.11   The triads notated here will be played in recording 10.11 so that you can memorize the difference in sound between consonant major and consonant minor triads. You will hear the major or minor quality of each triad identified, followed by the sound of the triad. After you have heard the triad, pause the recording so that you can assimilate the sound and its major or minor quality.

10.12 On recording 10.12 you will hear a major or a minor triad performed. After you have heard the triad, pause the recording so that you can identify it as major or minor. Next, release the pause and the triad will be played again and its quality identified so that you can check your answer. Twelve triads will be played; they are also identified in Appendix H.

 10.13 The triads notated here will be played on recording 10.13 so that you can memorize the difference in sound between dissonant diminished and dissonant augmented triads. You will hear the diminished or augmented quality of each triad identified, followed by the sound of the triad. After you have heard the triad, pause the recording so that you can assimilate the sound and its diminished or augmented quality.

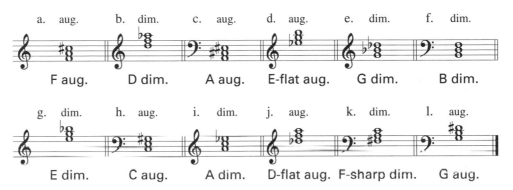

 10.14 On recording 10.14 you will hear a diminished or an augmented triad performed. After you have heard the triad, pause the recording so that you can identify it as diminished or augmented. Next, release the pause and the triad will be played again and its quality identified so that you can check your answer. Twelve triads will be played; they are also identified in Appendix H.

 10.15 Twenty-four triads will be performed on this recording. You will hear a major, a minor, a diminished, or an augmented triad played. After you have heard the triad, pause the recording so that you can identify the quality of the triad. Next, release the pause and the triad will be performed again and its quality identified so that you can check your answer. These triads are also identified in Appendix H.

TRIADS AND MAJOR SCALE RELATIONSHIPS

You may construct a triad on each degree of a major scale by using scale tones as roots, thirds, and fifths of the triad. Study the following examples.

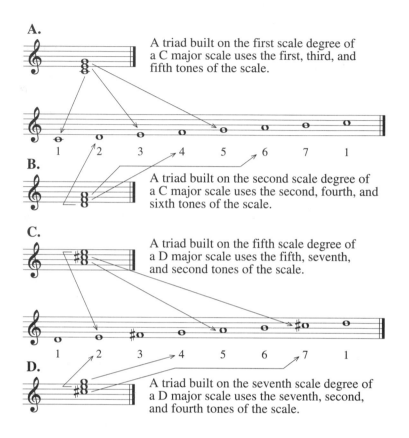

A. A triad built on the first scale degree of a C major scale uses the first, third, and fifth tones of the scale.

B. A triad built on the second scale degree of a C major scale uses the second, fourth, and sixth tones of the scale.

C. A triad built on the fifth scale degree of a D major scale uses the fifth, seventh, and second tones of the scale.

D. A triad built on the seventh scale degree of a D major scale uses the seventh, second, and fourth tones of the scale.

The root of a triad and its relationship to a key (scale) are indicated by a **roman numeral,** which represents the scale degree upon which the triad has been constructed. The quality of the triad is identified by the type of roman numeral: uppercase for major (I), lowercase for minor (ii), lowercase with the symbol ° for diminished (vii°), and uppercase with the symbol + for augmented (V+). Arabic numerals (1, 2, 3, etc.) will continue to be used to represent scale degrees.

If you analyze the triads constructed on each degree of any major scale, you will discover that major, minor, and diminished triads appear above the same scale degrees in all major keys: I, IV, and V triads are always major; ii, iii, and vi triads are always minor; and vii° triads are always diminished. *Memorize* Table 7 and study the following examples.

TABLE 7 Diatonic Triads in Major Keys	
Triad type	**Roman numeral symbol**
Major	I, IV, V
Minor	ii, iii, vi
Diminished	vii°
Augmented	none

Triads in C major

Roman numeral:	I	ii	iii	IV	V	vi	vii°
Triad name:	C maj.	D min.	E min.	F maj.	G maj.	A min.	B dim.

Triads in F major

Roman numeral:	I	ii	iii	IV	V	vi	vii°
Triad name:	F maj.	G min.	A min.	B-flat maj.	C maj.	D min.	E dim.

Identify the following triads and their relationship to the stated key by writing the chord number and the chord name below each triad (I, B-flat maj., etc.).

1. B-flat major

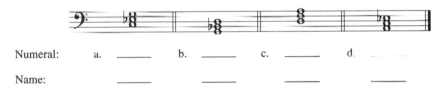

Numeral: a. _____   b. _____   c. _____   d. _____

Name: _____   _____   _____   _____

2. D major

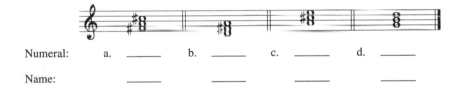

Numeral: a. _____   b. _____   c. _____   d. _____

Name: _____   _____   _____   _____

Write the following triads in the stated keys, and identify them by name (B-flat maj., D min., etc.).

1. G major

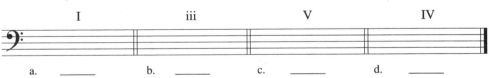

a. _____   b. _____   c. _____   d. _____

2. E-flat major

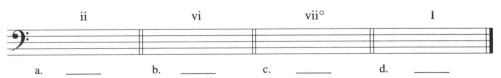

a. _____   b. _____   c. _____   d. _____

TRIADS AND MINOR SCALE RELATIONSHIPS

You may construct triads on each degree of a minor scale in the same manner you construct triads on major scale degrees. Because the whole-step–half-step formulas for the major and the three forms of the minor scales differ, the quality (major, minor, etc.) of the triads constructed on each scale degree may vary from one scale form to another. Study and compare the following triads found in the major, natural, harmonic, and melodic minor scales.

Triads in C major

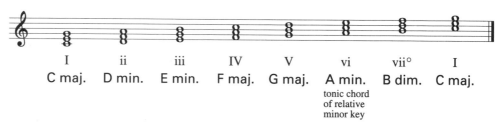

I	ii	iii	IV	V	vi	vii°	I
C maj.	D min.	E min.	F maj.	G maj.	A min.	B dim.	C maj.

vi: tonic chord of relative minor key

Triads in C natural minor

i	ii°	III	iv	v	VI	VII	i
C min.	D dim.	E-flat maj.	F min.	G min.	A-flat maj.	B-flat maj.	C min.

III: tonic chord of relative major key

VII: dominant of relative major key

Triads in C harmonic minor

i	ii°	III+	iv	V	VI	vii°	i
C min.	D dim.	E-flat aug.	F min.	G maj.	A-flat maj.	B dim.	C min.

Triads in C melodic minor, ascending pitches Triads constructed upon descending pitches of the melodic minor are the same as the triads in the natural minor scale.

i	ii	III+	IV	V	vi°	vii°	i
C min.	D min.	E-flat aug.	F maj.	G maj.	A dim.	B dim.	C min.

Because the natural, harmonic, and melodic minor scales include both major and minor sixth and seventh scale degrees, more than seven diatonic triads are possible. Study the following example, which shows all the triad possibilities in the minor mode. The underlined chords are most commonly used, and their roots and chord tones (except for the fifth of the III chord) are all pitches from the harmonic form of the minor scale. *Memorize* Table 8.

Triads in the C minor mode

   i   ii°   ii   III   III+   iv   IV   v   V   VI   vi°   VII   vii°

TABLE 8	Most Commonly Used Triads in Minor Keys	
Triad type	**Roman numeral symbol**	
Major	III, V, VI	
Minor	i, iv	
Diminished	ii°, vii°	
Augmented	none	

Identify the following triads and their relationship to the stated key by writing the chord number and the chord name below each triad (iv, D min., etc.).

1. A minor

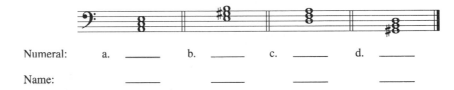

Numeral: a. _____   b. _____   c. _____   d. _____

Name: _____   _____   _____   _____

2. B minor

Numeral: a. _____   b. _____   c. _____   d. _____

Name: _____   _____   _____   _____

Write the following triads in the stated keys, and identify them by name (A min., B-flat maj., etc.).

1. C minor

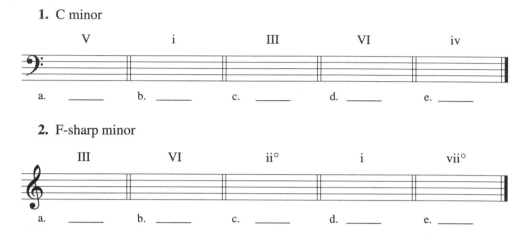

     V   i   III   VI   iv

a. _____ b. _____ c. _____ d. _____ e. _____

2. F-sharp minor

    III   VI   ii°   i   vii°

a. _____ b. _____ c. _____ d. _____ e. _____

SEVENTH CHORDS IN MAJOR AND MINOR KEYS

Triads in major and minor keys may be extended by adding a fourth tone, the interval of a seventh above the root. The resulting four-note chords are called **seventh chords,** and they are constructed with scale tones that form the root, third, fifth, and seventh of the chord. As with triads, the root and the key relationship of a seventh chord are identified by a roman numeral; the addition of an arabic numeral 7 signifies the tone a seventh above the root. The symbols M (major), $^\varnothing$ (half-diminished), and ° (diminished) are also used with the roman numeral when appropriate. There are five types of diatonic seventh chords in major and minor keys. Study and *memorize* Table 9.

TABLE 9   **Seventh-Chord Types in Major and Minor Keys**

Chord type	Roman numeral example
Major seventh (major triad plus major 7th)	I^{M7}
Dominant seventh (major triad plus minor 7th)	V^{7}
Minor seventh (minor triad plus minor 7th)	vi^{7}
Half-diminished seventh (diminished triad plus minor 7th)	$\text{ii}^{\varnothing 7}$
Diminished seventh (diminished triad plus diminished 7th)	$\text{vii}^{\circ 7}$

Diatonic Seventh Chords in Major Keys

Four of the five seventh-chord types occur as diatonic seventh chords in major keys. Study the following example and *memorize* Table 10.

Seventh chords in C major

| I^M7 | ii^7 | iii^7 | IV^M7 | V^7 | vi^7 | vii^ø7 |

TABLE 10   Diatonic Seventh Chords in Major Keys

Chord type	Roman numeral symbol
Major seventh	I^{M7}, IV^{M7}
Dominant seventh	V^{7}
Minor seventh	ii^{7}, iii^{7}, vi^{7}
Half-diminished seventh	$\text{vii}^{ø7}$
Diminished seventh	none

Diatonic Seventh Chords in Minor Keys

Because both the major and the minor sixth and seventh scale degrees are used in the minor mode, there are sixteen diatonic seventh-chord possibilities in minor keys. The following example shows the most commonly used seventh chords constructed on each scale degree. Notice that most chord tones are pitches from the harmonic form of the minor key. Study the example and *memorize* Table 11.

Most commonly used seventh chords in C minor

| i^7 | ii^ø7 | III^M7 | iv^7 | V^7 | VI^M7 | vi^ø7 | VII^7 | vii^°7 |

TABLE 11   Diatonic Seventh Chords in Minor Keys

Chord type	Roman numeral symbol	
Major seventh	III^{M7}, VI^{M7}	(III is the tonic of the relative major key.)
Dominant seventh	V^{7}, VII^{7}	(VII⁷ is the dom. 7th of the relative major key.)
Minor seventh	i^{7}, iv^{7}	
Half-diminished seventh	$\text{ii}^{ø7}$, $\text{vi}^{ø7}$	
Diminished seventh	$\text{vii}^{°7}$	

SCALE-DEGREE NAMES

The scale degrees of major and minor scales are often referred to by a set of traditional names rather than by numbers. These names, shown in the following example, are also used to identify chords, each name corresponding to the scale degree that serves as the root of the chord (e.g., I is the tonic chord, IV is the subdominant chord).

Study and *memorize* this example.

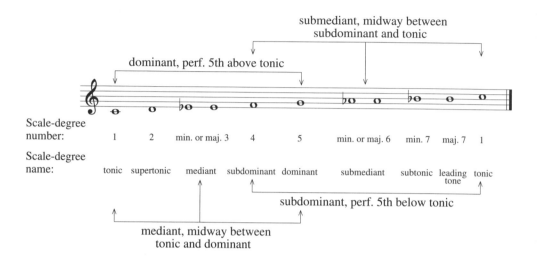

THE DOMINANT SEVENTH CHORD

The dominant chord, constructed on the fifth scale degree of a major or a minor key, appears more often as a seventh chord (V^7) than as a triad (V), for adding a tone a seventh above the root creates a sound with a much greater tendency to resolve to the tonic chord of the key. Because of its strong resolution to the tonic chord and because its unique sound is found in both major and minor keys **only** on the fifth (dominant) scale degree (see Table 10, page 129, and Table 11, page 129), **the dominant seventh chord is the most important chord used in tonal harmony to establish the major or minor tonality of a piece.**

Study the structure of the dominant seventh chords given in the following examples, and notice that the dominant seventh in minor uses the raised seventh scale degree from the harmonic minor form of the scale.

Dominant seventh chord in C major

Dominant seventh chord in D minor (harmonic)

Study exercises 10.16 and 10.17, each a comparison of a dominant triad resolved to a tonic triad and a dominant seventh chord resolved to the same tonic triad. The V^7-to-I is the stronger chord progression.

10.16   Perform these two chord progressions in C major.

10.17   Perform these two chord progressions in C minor (harmonic).

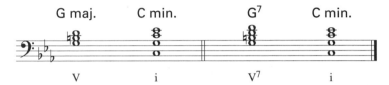

Identifying the Dominant Seventh Chord by Sound

The sound of the dominant seventh chord, like that of a diminished or an augmented triad, is dissonant. In fact, the third, fifth, and seventh chord tones of the dominant seventh chord form a diminished triad; therefore, the dominant seventh chord has the tritone dissonances (third-to-seventh chord tones) as part of its overall sound. Because of its unique restless quality, this important chord is easily identified when heard. Perform example 10.18 and *memorize* the unique dominant seventh sound.

10.18   a. Dom. 7th in the key of D major or minor   b. Dom. 7th in the key of G major or minor   c. Dom. 7th in the key of C major or minor

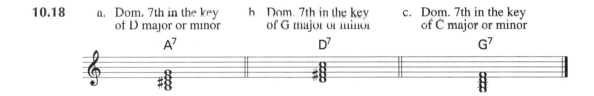

TRIAD INVERSIONS

Triads do not always occur in music with the root sounding as the lowest of the three pitches. Sometimes the third or the fifth of the triad will be used as the lowest pitch so that a better bass line will be created to complement the melody. When that is the case, the triad is said to be in an **inverted position.**

Triads may appear in three positions: **root position,** with the root as the lowest pitch; **first inversion,** with the third as the lowest pitch; and **second inversion,** with the fifth as the lowest pitch. Whereas a triad's relationship to a given key is represented by roman numerals, inversions are indicated by arabic numerals that identify the interval between the bass note and the inverted chord tones. When the roman numeral is written alone (I, V, etc.), root position is indicated; when the roman numeral is followed by an arabic 6 (I^6, V^6, etc.), first inversion is indicated; and when the roman numeral is followed by the arabic numerals $^6_4$ (I^6_4, V^6_4, etc.), second inversion is indicated. Study and perform the following examples. Then *memorize* this information.

10.19   Key of C major

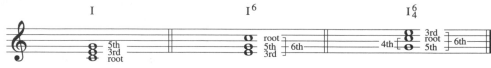

C maj. triad in root position | C maj. triad in 1st inversion (3rd in bass) | C maj. triad in 2nd inversion (5th in bass)

10.20   Key of D minor

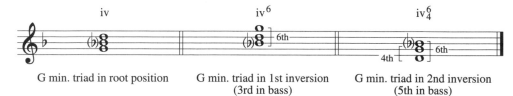

G min. triad in root position | G min. triad in 1st inversion (3rd in bass) | G min. triad in 2nd inversion (5th in bass)

Write and perform the following triads.

1. E major in

Root position   1st inversion   2nd inversion

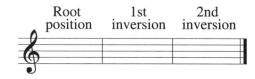

2. B-flat minor in

Root position   1st inversion   2nd inversion

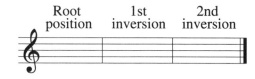

3. A diminished in

Root position   1st inversion   2nd inversion

4. D-flat augmented in

Root position   1st inversion   2nd inversion

Write, identify, and perform the following triads (e.g., C maj., 1st inversion; D min., 2nd inversion).

1. In the key of B-flat major

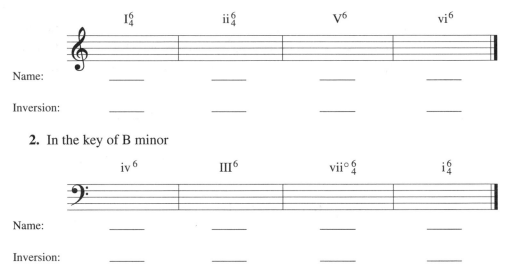

Name: _____   _____   _____   _____

Inversion: _____   _____   _____   _____

2. In the key of B minor

Name: _____   _____   _____   _____

Inversion: _____   _____   _____   _____

SEVENTH-CHORD INVERSIONS

Seventh chords may appear in three inversions as well as in root position. When the roman numeral is followed by an arabic ^{7} (I^{M7}, i^7, V^7, etc.), **root position** is indicated; when the roman numeral is followed by an arabic $^6_5$ (IV^{M6}_5, iv^6_5, V^6_5, etc.), **first inversion** is indicated; when the roman numeral is followed by an arabic $^4_3$ (ii^4_3, V^4_3, etc.), **second inversion** is indicated; and when the roman numeral is followed by an arabic ^{2} (I^{M2}, i^2, V^2, etc.), **third inversion** is indicated. Study and perform the following examples. Then *memorize* Table 12 (page 134).

10.21   Key of G major

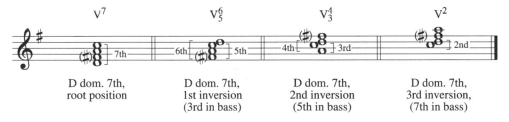

D dom. 7th,	D dom. 7th,	D dom. 7th,	D dom. 7th,
root position	1st inversion	2nd inversion	3rd inversion,
	(3rd in bass)	(5th in bass)	(7th in bass)

10.22   Key of F minor

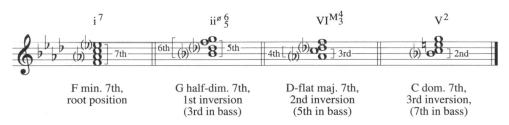

F min. 7th,	G half-dim. 7th,	D-flat maj. 7th,	C dom. 7th,
root position	1st inversion	2nd inversion	3rd inversion,
	(3rd in bass)	(5th in bass)	(7th in bass)

TABLE 12   Inversion Symbols for Triads and Seventh Chords

Bass note	Triad symbol (example)	Seventh-chord symbol (example)
Root position (root in bass)	Roman numeral alone (I)	Roman numeral with arabic ^{7} (I^{M7})
First inversion (3rd in bass)	Roman numeral with arabic ^{6} (V^6)	Roman numeral with arabic $^6_5$ (V^6_5)
Second inversion (5th in bass)	Roman numeral with arabic $^6_4$ (vi^6_4)	Roman numeral with arabic $^4_3$ (vi^4_3)
Third inversion (7th in bass)	None	Roman numeral with arabic ^{2} ($ii^{\varnothing 2}$)

Write, identify, and perform the following seventh chords (e.g., G dom. 7th, 1st inversion; E min. 7th, 3rd inversion).

1. In the key of E-flat major

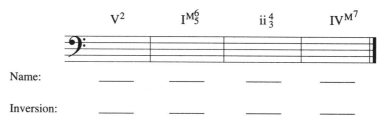

V^7 V^6_5 V^4_3 V^2

Name: ____   ____   ____   ____

Inversion: ____   ____   ____   ____

2. In the key of F-sharp major

V^2 I^{M6}_5 ii^4_3 IV^{M7}

Name: ____   ____   ____   ____

Inversion: ____   ____   ____   ____

3. In the key of A minor

V^4_3 V^6_5 V^7 V^2

Name: ____   ____   ____   ____

Inversion: ____   ____   ____   ____

4. In the key of B minor

V^6_5 i^7 $vii^{\circ 2}$ VI^{M4}_3

Name: ____   ____   ____   ____

Inversion: ____   ____   ____   ____

USING PRIMARY CHORDS TO HARMONIZE SIMPLE MELODIES IN MAJOR AND MINOR KEYS

Chords constructed on the tonic (first scale degree), the subdominant (fourth scale degree), and the dominant (fifth scale degree) of a major or a minor key include *all* seven of the scale tones. These three chords are the *primary chords* of tonal music, and they are used most often to harmonize music in major and minor keys. You have already studied and learned to sing and play these three chords as arpeggios in Chapter 8. Turn to page 87, and review the information regarding primary chords; then perform singing drill E.

When a series of chords is performed in a sequence with each chord progressing to the next, the resulting harmonic series is called a **chord progression.** Study and learn to play the following two chord progressions. The first progression uses the primary chords in C major: I, C major in root position; IV_4^6, F major in second inversion; and V_5^6, G dominant seventh in first inversion with the fifth of the chord (D) not being played. The second progression uses the primary chords in C minor (harmonic form) with the same progression and chord inversions: i, iv_4^6, V_5^6.

Play these chord progressions over and over, using the left-hand fingering given. Practice them until you can hear in your mind the sound of each chord and the sound created by the interaction of the chords as they move in succession from one to another. With repeated practice you will develop *muscle memory* that will enable your hand to move automatically to the chord you are hearing. Once you can play these progressions in C major and C minor, transpose them to, and learn to play them in, other major and minor keys. See Appendix G for additional chord accompaniment patterns.

Chord progression in C major

Chord progression in C minor (harmonic)

After you have developed some proficiency playing these two chord progressions, begin to improvise different chord sequences using the three primary chords. The I (i) chord may move to the IV (iv), the V, or the V^7; the IV (iv) chord may move to the I (i), the V, or the V^7; the V or V^7 moves most often to I, but in popular and folk music styles the V or V^7 occasionally moves to the IV (iv). Use your *ears* to help you make good musical choices when improvising chord progressions. More information about chord progressions and harmonic cadences will be presented in following chapters.

Next, with your right hand add improvised melodies to the chord progressions you play with your left hand. Again use your ears to help you choose melody tones that work well with the accompanying chords. Create your melodies using the same scale tones used to create the chord progressions. When your melody is disjunct (skipping), **harmonic tones** (pitches that match the accompanying chord tones) are your best choice (see *Just Sing It!,* page 2, phrases A1 and A2). When your melody moves up or down the scale (diatonically), some of the pitches will be **nonharmonic tones,** or **nonchord tones.** These nonharmonic tones do not match any of the accompanying chord tones and sound dissonant against the harmony. The dissonant nonharmonic tones are most often placed on the weak part of the meter beats (see *Just Sing It!*, page 2, ending). More information regarding nonharmonic tones will be presented in the following chapters. For now, use your ears and play what sounds good to you.

Study the songs *Just Sing It!* (page 2), *Early One Morning* (page 78), and *Joshua Fought the Battle of Jericho* (page 78) for more information regarding the key, the chord progression, and the use of harmonic tones and nonharmonic tones. Sing each of these songs as you play a left-hand chord accompaniment; then play the melody with the right hand as you play a left-hand chord accompaniment.

ASSIGNMENT

1. Identify the following intervals; then notate the inversion of each interval in the blank measure, and identify it.

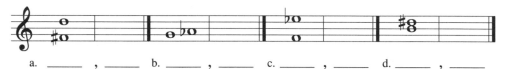

 a. _____ , _____   b. _____ , _____   c. _____ , _____   d. _____ , _____

2. Identify the following chords and the root position or inversion of each (e.g., F maj., root position; B min., 1st inversion).

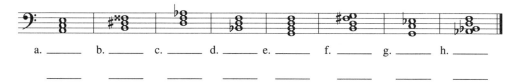

 a. _____   b. _____   c. _____   d. _____   e. _____   f. _____   g. _____   h. _____

 _____   _____   _____   _____   _____   _____   _____   _____

3. Write the following chords in the stated keys, and identify them (e.g., A maj., root position; B min. 7th, 2nd inversion).

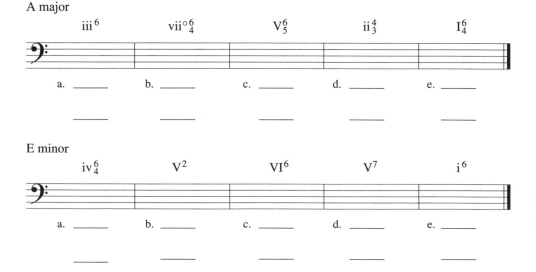

A major

   iii^6 vii$^{\circ 6}_4$ V$^6_5$ ii$^4_3$ I$^6_4$

 a. _____   b. _____   c. _____   d. _____   e. _____

 _____   _____   _____   _____   _____

E minor

   iv$^6_4$ V^2 VI^6 V^7 i^6

 a. _____   b. _____   c. _____   d. _____   e. _____

 _____   _____   _____   _____   _____

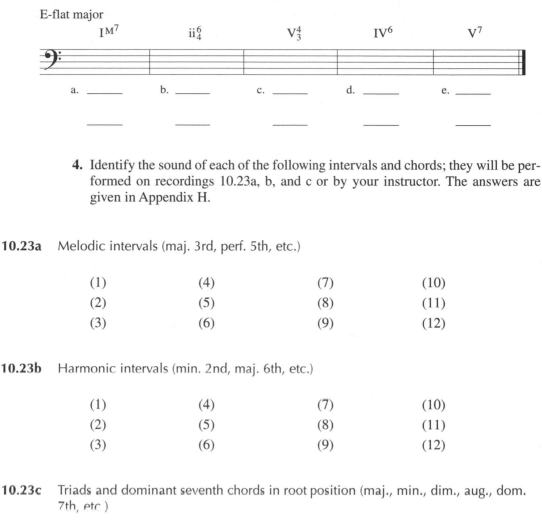

E-flat major

I M⁷   ii⁶₄   V⁴₃   IV⁶   V⁷

a. _____   b. _____   c. _____   d. _____   e. _____

_____   _____   _____   _____   _____

4. Identify the sound of each of the following intervals and chords; they will be performed on recordings 10.23a, b, and c or by your instructor. The answers are given in Appendix H.

10.23a   Melodic intervals (maj. 3rd, perf. 5th, etc.)

(1)	(4)	(7)	(10)
(2)	(5)	(8)	(11)
(3)	(6)	(9)	(12)

10.23b   Harmonic intervals (min. 2nd, maj. 6th, etc.)

(1)	(4)	(7)	(10)
(2)	(5)	(8)	(11)
(3)	(6)	(9)	(12)

10.23c   Triads and dominant seventh chords in root position (maj., min., dim., aug., dom. 7th, etc.)

(1)	(4)	(7)	(10)
(2)	(5)	(8)	(11)
(3)	(6)	(9)	(12)

5. Notate a four-measure melody in F major; it will be performed on recording 10.24 or by your instructor. The notation of this melody is written in Appendix H.

10.24

6. Create a simple piano accompaniment for your *Original Melody No. 2* (page 97) using the primary chords I, IV⁶₄, V⁶₅. Use the following procedures.

   a. Learn to play the primary chord progression presented on page 135 in the same major key that you used to write *Original Melody No. 2.*

   b. Play your melody on the piano very slowly with the right hand. As you play, listen to hear which primary-chord sound the melody suggests; play that chord with your left hand. Be patient; try each of the three chords until your *ear* tells you which chord works best with each measure of your piece. Keep trying to find the best match of melody and chords, and you will soon learn to harmonize melodies easily.

c. Notate your melody on the staves provided below, and write the chord symbols above the melody where each chord is to be played.

d. Choose one of the accompaniment patterns from Appendix G, and practice your piece until you can give a musical performance.

e. Perform your piece for friends or classmates.

ORIGINAL MELODY NO. 2
IN MAJOR WITH CHORD ACCOMPANIMENT

7. Create a simple piano accompaniment for your *Original Melody No. 3* (page 116) using the primary chords i, iv$^6_4$, V$^6_5$. Use the same procedures given in 6a–e.

ORIGINAL MELODY NO. 3
IN MINOR WITH CHORD ACCOMPANIMENT

chapter 11

More Meter and Rhythm Possibilities

MULTIMETRIC COMPOSITIONS

Although it is common for a music composition to remain in the same meter from beginning to end, some pieces change meter once, twice, or many times. This is done to achieve the special effect that only changing the metric accent can produce. If a piece includes meter changes, it is a **multimetric** or **mixed meter** composition. Study and perform the following multimetric rhythm examples, accenting (>) the first beat of each measure.[1] Notice that the new meter signature is placed in the first measure where the meter change occurs.

11.1 **Moderato**

11.2 **Moderato**

$\frac{5}{4}$ METER

If you want to achieve the effect of alternating duple and triple meter in every other measure, you may either write a multimetric piece alternating $\frac{2}{4}$ meter and $\frac{3}{4}$ meter or use $\frac{5}{4}$ meter (2 beats + 3 beats = 5 beats) throughout the piece. Study and perform the following examples. Notice that the meter beats for $\frac{5}{4}$ meter fall into two groups, either 2 beats + 3 beats (example A.2) or 3 beats + 2 beats (example B.2). Also notice that the multimetric and $\frac{5}{4}$ examples are rhythmically the same.

[1]This accent mark (>) indicates the stress of one tone over others.

140

A.

    1. Alternating $\frac{2}{4}$ and $\frac{3}{4}$ meters

Moderato

    2. $\frac{5}{4}$ meter (2 beats + 3 beats)

Moderato

B.

    1. Alternating $\frac{3}{4}$ and $\frac{2}{4}$ meters

Moderato

    2. $\frac{5}{4}$ meter (3 beats + 2 beats)

Moderato

$\frac{7}{4}$ METER

$\frac{7}{4}$ meter is felt as one of several meter groupings: 3 beats + 4 beats, 4 beats + 3 beats, 3 beats + 2 beats + 2 beats, 2 beats + 2 beats + 3 beats, or 2 beats + 3 beats + 2 beats. Study and perform the following multimetric and $\frac{7}{4}$ meter examples. Notice that the multimetric and $\frac{7}{4}$ meter examples are rhythmically the same.

C.

    1. Alternating $\frac{3}{4}$ and $\frac{4}{4}$ meters

Moderato

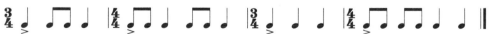

    2. $\frac{7}{4}$ meter (3 beats + 4 beats)

Moderato

D.

1. Multimetric

Moderato

2. ⁷⁄₄ meter (4 + 3 and 2 + 2 + 3)

Moderato

²⁄₂ AND ¢ METERS

²⁄₂ is a simple duple meter that uses the half note (♩) as the beat unit. The **alla breve** sign, ¢, indicates a quick duple meter with the half note as the beat unit; it may be used in place of the ²⁄₂ meter signature. *Alla breve* is also known as **cut time.**

²⁄₂ is called "two two meter" or "two two time."	2 = duple meter, two beats per measure 2 = half note receives one beat
¢ is called "*alla breve* meter," "*alla breve* time," or "cut time."	¢ = duple meter, two beats per measure and half note receives one beat

Study the following note values in ²⁄₂ and ¢ meters. Remember that the 2:1 ratio relationship of rhythm symbols is constant, regardless of the meter.

Study and perform the following examples.[2]

    11.3

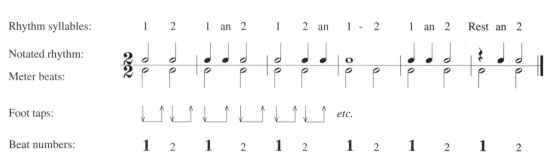

---

[2]See Appendixes A, C, and E for additional examples in ²⁄₂ and ¢ meters.

11.4

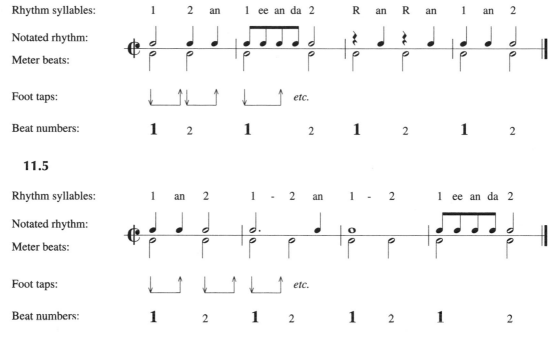

11.5

³⁄₈ METER

³⁄₈ meter is a simple triple meter that uses the eighth note as the beat unit.

| ³⁄₈ is called "three eight meter" or "three eight time." | 3 = triple meter, three beats per measure
8 = eighth note receives one beat |

Study the following note values in ³⁄₈ meter. Remember that the 2:1 ratio relationship of rhythm symbols is constant, regardless of the meter.

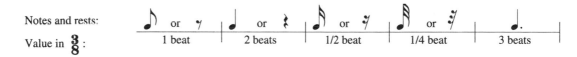

Study and perform the following examples.[3]

11.6

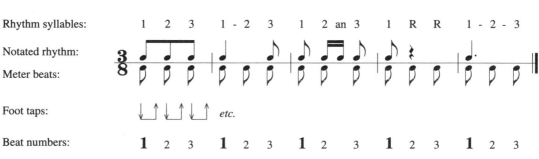

[3]See Appendixes A and E for additional exercises in ³⁄₈ meter.

11.7

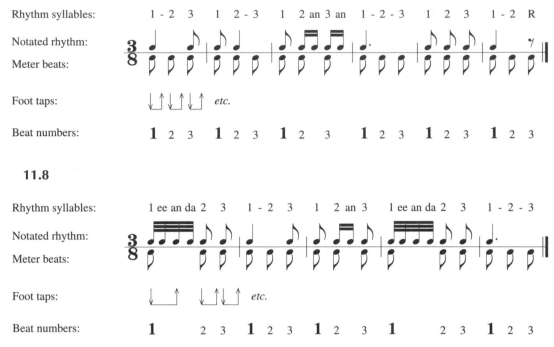

Rhythm syllables:	1 - 2 3	1 2 - 3	1 2 an 3 an	1 - 2 - 3	1 2 3	1 - 2 R
Notated rhythm:						
Meter beats:						

Foot taps: ↓↑↓↑↓↑ *etc.*

Beat numbers: **1** 2 3 **1** 2 3 **1** 2 3 **1** 2 3 **1** 2 3 **1** 2 3

11.8

Rhythm syllables:	1 ee an da 2 3	1 - 2 3	1 2 an 3	1 ee an da 2 3	1 - 2 - 3
Notated rhythm:					
Meter beats:					

Foot taps: ↓ ↑ ↓↑↓↑ *etc.*

Beat numbers: **1** 2 3 **1** 2 3 **1** 2 3 **1** 2 3 **1** 2 3

COMPOUND METERS

Simple meters use simple notes (notes without a dot ♩ ♪ ♫, etc.) to represent the meter beat, and each beat and its representative note can be subdivided into two equal
parts and the parts further divided into four parts, eight parts, and so on. **Compound
meters** use compound notes (notes with a dot ♩. ♪. ♫., etc.) to represent the meter
beat, and each beat and its representative note can be subdivided into *three* equal parts
and the parts further divided into six parts, twelve parts, and so on. Study, listen to, and
compare examples 11.9 and 11.10. Then play these two examples on a keyboard instrument, performing the meter beats as you play and sing the subdivisions of
each beat.

11.9 Simple duple meter

duple subdivision

Sing and play on piano,
right-hand pitch G:

Play on piano,
left-hand pitch C:

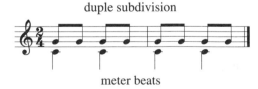

meter beats

11.10 Compound duple meter

triple subdivision

Sing and play on piano,
right-hand pitch G:

Play on piano,
left-hand pitch C:

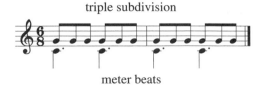

meter beats

Compound meter signatures are derived from simple meter signatures by multiplying the top numeral of a simple meter signature by three. Study and *memorize* Table 13.

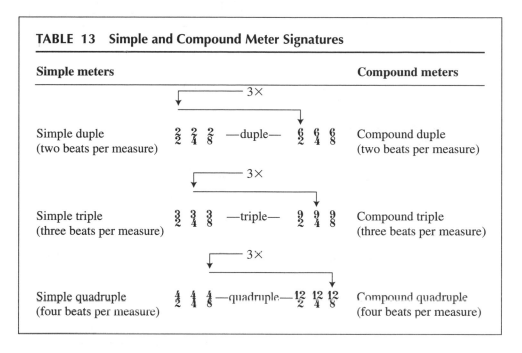

TABLE 13   Simple and Compound Meter Signatures

In addition to the compound meters in Table 13, music in simple triple meters ($\frac{3}{2}$, $\frac{3}{4}$, $\frac{3}{8}$) may be felt and performed like compound meters when the quickness of tempo necessitates a performance in which one compound beat is felt in each measure instead of three simple beats per measure. For example, waltzes and scherzo movements demand a quick triple meter that is performed with one beat per measure, each beat being divisible into three subdivisions.

Study examples 11.11 through 11.19. Then perform these compound duple, triple, and quadruple meter pieces. Sing the rhythm notated on the pitch G as you perform both the rhythm and the meter beats on the piano.[4]

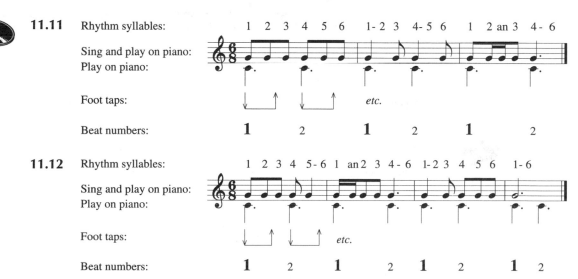

[4]See Appendixes A, C, and E for additional exercises in $\frac{6}{8}$, $\frac{9}{8}$, and $\frac{12}{8}$ meters.

11.13

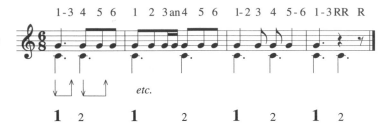

11.14

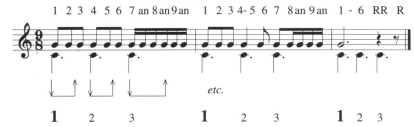

11.15

11.16

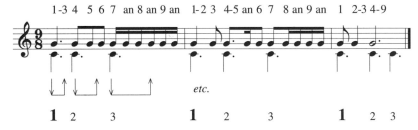

11.17

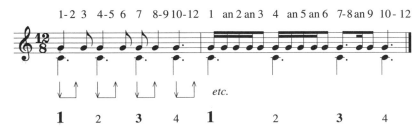

11.18

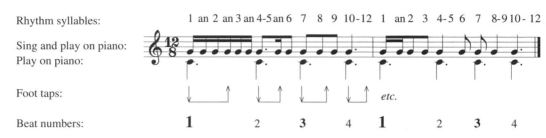

| Rhythm syllables: | 1 an 2 an 3 an 4-5 an 6 7 8 9 10-12 1 an 2 3 4-5 6 7 8-9 10-12 |

Sing and play on piano:
Play on piano:

Foot taps: *etc.*

Beat numbers: 1 2 3 4 1 2 3 4

11.19

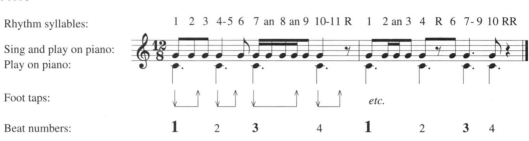

Rhythm syllables: 1 2 3 4-5 6 7 an 8 an 9 10-11 R 1 2 an 3 4 R 6 7-9 10 RR

Sing and play on piano:
Play on piano:

Foot taps: *etc.*

Beat numbers: 1 2 3 4 1 2 3 4

BORROWED RHYTHM PATTERNS

When you are creating a piece in a particular meter but momentarily wish to use a rhythm pattern common to another meter, you may do so without changing the meter signature by using a borrowed rhythm pattern. For example, if you want a triple division of the beat in a simple meter where the common division is duple, then the triple division common to compound meter must be borrowed. Likewise, if you want a duple division of the beat in a compound meter, you must borrow it from a simple meter. Study and perform the following examples.

Eighth-Note Triplet
Three equal notes in the time of one beat; used in simple meter and borrowed from compound meter

Eighth-Note Duplet
Two equal notes in the time of one beat; used in compound meter and borrowed from simple meter

Sixteenth-Note Sextuplet
Six equal notes in the time of one beat; used in simple meter and borrowed from compound meter

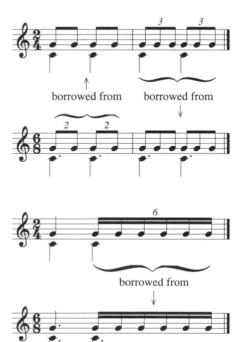

Sixeenth-Note Quadruplet
Four equal notes in the time of one beat; used in compound meter and borrowed from simple meter

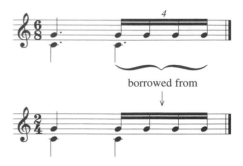

IRREGULAR RHYTHM PATTERNS

Although one, two, three, four, six, and eight equal notes to one beat may be notated in the simple and compound meters by using regular and borrowed rhythm patterns, irregular rhythm patterns must be used to notate five, seven, and nine equal notes to one beat.

Quintuplet
Five equal notes in one beat

Septuplet
Seven equal notes in one beat

Nontuplet
Nine equal notes in one beat

There are many rhythm syllable methods used to count borrowed and irregular rhythm patterns. The following is one method. Use any method that works well for you. Study and perform these examples.

 11.20

Rhythm syllables: 1   2 an   1 T L 2 T L   1   1 2 3 4 5 6   1 an 1 2 3 4 5   1   R
                                   (1 Trip Let 2 Trip Let)

 11.21

Rhythm syllables: 1   2   3   4 - 6   1   an   2   an   1 - 3   1 2 3 4   1 - 3   4   5   6

Study and perform the following rhythm studies, which use borrowed and irregular rhythm patterns.[5]

---

[5]See Appendixes A, C, and E for additional practice in performing borrowed and irregular rhythm patterns.

SYNCOPATED RHYTHMS

When the natural accent that falls on the downbeat is displaced by a rhythm pattern that accents the upbeat, the rhythm pattern is referred to as a **syncopated rhythm.** Study and perform examples 11.22 through 11.24.

 11.22

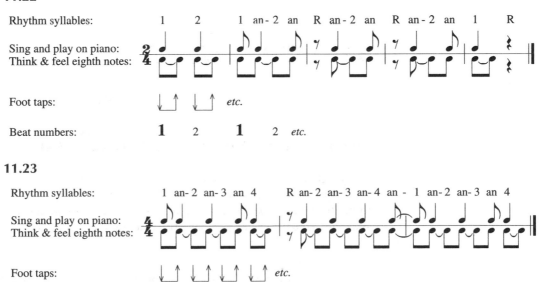

11.23

11.24

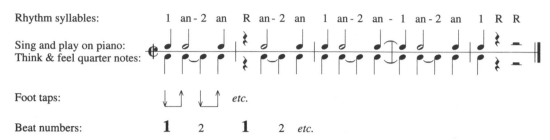

Study and perform the following rhythm studies, which use syncopated rhythms.[6]

RHYTHMS RELATED TO THE ♩♩♩ AND ♪♪♪♪ PATTERNS

Many different rhythm patterns may be created by tying various notes within the triplet or four-sixteenth-note pattern. To understand and perform these rhythms related to the triplet and sixteenth-note patterns, you must think and feel the basic triplet or sixteenth-note pattern as you perform. Study the following examples.

[6]See Appendixes A and C for additional practice in performing syncopated rhythms.

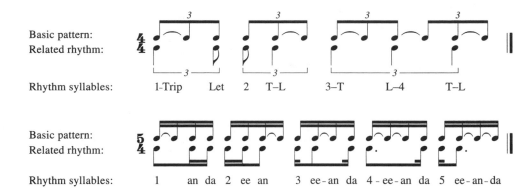

Study, listen to, and perform examples 11.25 through 11.27.

11.25

11.26

11.27

Study and perform the following rhythm studies, which use rhythms related to the triplet and the four-sixteenth-note patterns.[7]

1.

2.

3.

4.

[7]See Appendixes A, C, and E for additional practice in performing rhythms related to the triplet and four-sixteenth-note patterns.

5.

6.

ASSIGNMENT

1. Define the following meter signatures.

   a. $\frac{2}{4}$

   b. $\frac{5}{4}$

   c. $\frac{7}{4}$

   d. ¢

   e. $\frac{6}{8}$

   f. $\frac{9}{8}$

   g. $\frac{12}{8}$

2. Explain in your own terms the difference in the natural subdivision of the beat in simple meter and compound meter.

3. Which of these meters is a compound duple meter?
   $\frac{3}{4}$ $\frac{2}{8}$ $\frac{6}{8}$ $\frac{4}{2}$ _____

4. Which of these meters is a compound triple meter?
   $\frac{9}{4}$ $\frac{4}{2}$ $\frac{4}{8}$ $\frac{2}{8}$ _____

5. Which of these meters is a compound quadruple meter?
   $\frac{6}{4}$ $\frac{9}{2}$ $\frac{3}{4}$ $\frac{4}{8}$ $\frac{12}{8}$ _____

6. Explain in your own terms the concept of borrowed rhythm patterns.

7. Define the following terms.

   a. Rhythm syncopation

   b. *Pianissimo* (***pp***)

   c. *Fortissimo* (***ff***)

   d. *Alla breve*

   e. *Mezzo forte* (***mf***)

   f. *Mezzo piano* (***mp***)

8. Define *multimetric* and explain its use in a music composition.

9. Write rhythm syllables above the following exercises. Also write an accent (>) below the notes in each measure that coincide with the primary and secondary accents of the meter.

a.

b.

c.

d.

e.

f.

g.

h.

i.

j.

10. Perform rhythm exercises 9a–9r.

11. Perform additional rhythm exercises in Appendixes A and C, and melodic exercises in Appendix E.

12. Practice improvising rhythm pieces in compound meters ($^6_8$, $^9_8$, $^{12}_8$).

13. Practice improvising melodies in compound meters ($^6_8$, $^9_8$, $^{12}_8$) using different major and minor keys.

14. Create, notate, and perform a sixteen-measure melody with a four-measure introduction and a four-measure ending (twenty-four measures total). This melody should be written in $^6_8$ meter, and you may choose any major or minor key. Use the following procedures.

   a. Use the same procedures you followed in Chapters 8 and 9 to create your *Original Melody No. 2* and *Original Melody No. 3*.

b. Create a harmonized accompaniment for your melody by using the same procedures you followed in Chapter 10 to harmonize *Original Melody No. 2* and *Original Melody No. 3*.

c. Notate your melody on the staves provided below, and write the chord symbols above the melody where each chord is to be played.

d. Choose one of the accompaniment patterns from Appendix G, and practice your piece until you can give a musical performance.

e. Perform your piece for friends or classmates.

ORIGINAL MELODY NO. 4
IN $\frac{6}{8}$ METER WITH CHORD ACCOMPANIMENT

chapter 12

Chord Progressions in Major and Minor Keys

PRIMARY AND SECONDARY CHORD FUNCTIONS

In Chapter 10 you learned how chords are constructed on each pitch of major and minor scales. You also learned how to use the three primary chords of a key to create harmonic accompaniments for major and minor melodies (major: I, IV, V; minor: i, iv, V). The following information, although only introductory in its depth, will help you understand how all the chords in major and minor keys work together to create a wide choice of harmonic colors with which to harmonize your original compositions.

The **secondary chords** in major and minor keys are constructed on the second third, sixth, and seventh scale degrees (major: ii, iii, vi, vii°; minor: ii°, III, VI, vii°). Because melodies that use only the seven pitches of a major or a minor scale may be harmonized by using only the primary chords, it is not necessary to use the secondary chords to harmonize major or minor melodies unless you want more variety in your harmonizations. Having already learned to hear and perform primary chords as they function within chord progressions, you can easily learn to hear and perform the secondary chords as they function within the key by thinking of the secondary chords as substitutions for the primary chords.

Study and *memorize* the sounds of the following cadences and chord progressions by learning to play them on a keyboard instrument. After you have learned to play the chord progressions in the keys of C major and C minor, transpose them and learn to play them in all keys. Also learn to play these progressions using the accompaniment patterns presented in Appendix G.

AUTHENTIC AND PLAGAL CADENCES

A **cadence** may be thought of as a harmonic goal, a point of harmonic rest. Although the ultimate harmonic goal is the final cadence on the tonic chord, there are many cadences within each piece. They occur at the ends of phrases, and they may come to rest on the tonic chord or on chords other than the tonic. The **authentic cadence** (V–I; V–i) and the **plagal cadence** (IV–I; iv–i) are the two most widely used cadences. Notice that these two cadences use the three primary chords (I, IV, V; i, iv, V).

A. Authentic cadences

12.1a Authentic cadence V⁷–I Strongest cadence for establishing major key. Use left-hand fingering given next to notation.

C major: I   V⁶₅   I

12.1b Authentic cadence V⁷–i Strongest cadence for establishing minor key.

C minor: i   V⁶₅   i

B. Plagal cadences

12.2a Plagal cadence IV–I Weaker cadence for establishing major key. Hymnlike cadence, "Amen."

C major: I   IV⁶₄   I

12.2b Plagal cadence iv–i Weaker cadence for establishing minor key.

C minor: i   iv⁶₄   i

CHORD SUBSTITUTIONS AND FREQUENTLY USED CHORD PROGRESSIONS

The following secondary chords may be substituted for primary chords to create additional harmonic interest without disturbing the harmonic function of the progression.

A. The vii° chord may be substituted for the V⁷ chord in both major and minor keys. However, the authentic cadence V⁷–I or V⁷–i establishes the tonality more strongly than the substitution cadence vii°–I or vii°–i. Authentic cadences are therefore used more frequently.

12.3a   C major: I   V$_5^6$ I

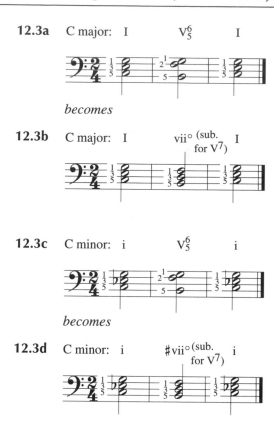

becomes

12.3b   C major: I   vii° (sub. for V^7)   I

12.3c   C minor: i   V$_5^6$ i

becomes

12.3d   C minor: i   #vii° (sub. for V^7)   i

B. The ii (ii°) chord is often substituted for the IV (iv) chord in both major and minor keys.

12.4a   C major: I   IV$_4^6$ V$_5^6$ I

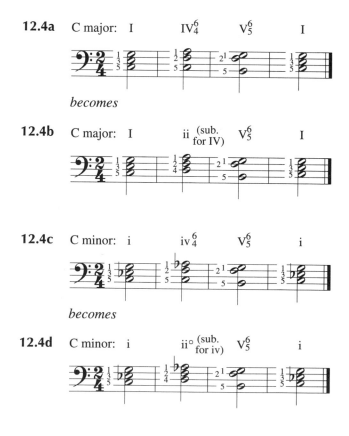

becomes

12.4b   C major: I   ii (sub. for IV)   V$_5^6$ I

12.4c   C minor: i   iv$_4^6$ V$_5^6$ i

becomes

12.4d   C minor: i   ii° (sub. for iv)   V$_5^6$ i

C. The vi (vi°) chord is often substituted for the I (i) chord in both major and minor keys.

becomes

becomes

D. The iii (III) chord may substitute for the I (i) chord in both major and minor keys.

CHORD ROOT MOVEMENTS WITHIN HARMONIC PROGRESSIONS

The root movements of chords within harmonic progressions in major and minor keys may be understood and heard more easily if they are reduced to *only three basic intervals:* the progression of a fifth (its inversion, the fourth), the progression of a second (its inversion, the seventh), and the progression of a third (its inversion, the sixth).

Chord Progressions with Root Movements by Fifths

Chord progressions with root movements by descending fifths create the strongest harmonic movement in major and minor tonalities. Therefore, the most widely used interval for chord root movements in tonal music is the descending fifth, perfect or diminished, and its inversion the ascending fourth, perfect or augmented. Study the following major and minor chord progressions, which begin on the tonic chord (I or i), progress to the subdominant (IV or iv), and continue the sequence of fifths with a cadence on the tonic (I–IV–vii°–iii–vi–ii–V–I). Similar chord progressions may begin on the tonic chord, skip to *any* chord in this sequence, and progress by fifths to a cadence on the tonic (I–ii–V–I; I–vi–ii–V–I; etc.). In addition, chord progressions may begin on any chord in this sequence and progress by fifths to a cadence on the tonic (vi–ii–V^7–I; ii–V^7–I; etc.).

Study and learn to perform the following chord progressions. You may find it helpful to think of these root movements by fifths as moving around the Circle of Fifths presented on page 74.

Chord Progressions with Root Movements by Seconds

Chord progressions with root movements by ascending or descending seconds also create strong harmonic sequences in both major and minor keys.

Study and learn to perform the following chord progressions. Root movements by seconds are indicated with the sign ⌐⌐. These examples are notated on previous pages.

(12.4a) I IV V^7 I

(12.4b) I ii V^7 I

(12.6b) I iii IV V^7 I

(12.6e) I iii vi V^7 I

(12.3b) I vii° I

Chord Progressions with Root Movements by Thirds

Chord progressions with root movements by ascending or descending thirds create weak harmonic sequences because chords with roots a third apart share two common chord tones. Study the following examples, and notice that the shared common chord tones create a smooth, subtle harmonic change, even though the qualities change between major and minor.

Study and learn to perform the following chord progressions. Root movements by thirds are indicated with the sign ⌐—. These examples are notated on previous pages.

(12.5b) I vi IV V⁷ I

(12.6b) I iii IV V⁷ I

HARMONIZING MELODIES USING PRIMARY AND SECONDARY CHORDS

In Chapter 10 you learned to harmonize melodies using the primary chords (major: I, IV, V; minor: i, iv, V). In this chapter you have studied the secondary chords (major: ii, iii, vi, vii°; minor: ii°, III, VI, vii°) and how they can be substituted for the primary chords to achieve a greater variety of chord progressions. Now you can begin to harmonize melodies using all the chords available in major and minor keys.

Practice the chord progressions introduced in this chapter until you have memorized the sound of each progression. Then practice improvising melodies in the right hand that sound good with the chords you are playing in the left hand. Most of your melody pitches should match one of the tones used in the accompanying chord, but nonchord tones may also be used. Nonchord tones usually occur between two chord tones. They may appear in scale passages moving up or down, or a nonchord tone may be approached by a leap and then resolved up or down to a chord tone. Several nonchord tones sounding in a sequence should be avoided, for they will create a dissonant passage that will usually sound like "wrong notes" to the listener.

After you have practiced improvising melodies above a predetermined chord progression, practice improvising chord progressions that will accompany simple melodies that are familiar to you. Remember, any melody in a major or a minor key may be harmonized using only the primary chords. First, harmonize a familiar melody using only the primary chords; then create a more interesting harmonic accompaniment by including secondary as well as primary chords in your chord progression. Listen closely as you try different chords and your ears will help you choose chord progressions that sound good with the melody. Don't get discouraged! It takes repeated practice to develop the skills necessary to hear and perform chord progressions and melodies that work well together.

Study, listen to, and learn to perform *Just Sing It!* notated in example 12.9. Compare this version, which uses secondary as well as primary chords for the harmonic accompaniment, with version 1.1 (page 2), which uses only primary chords for the accompaniment. Notice that in version 12.9 some of the melody pitches have become nonharmonic tones.

 12.9

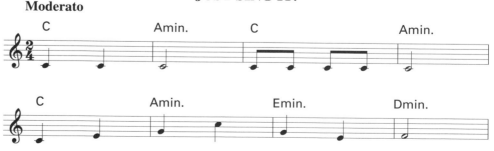

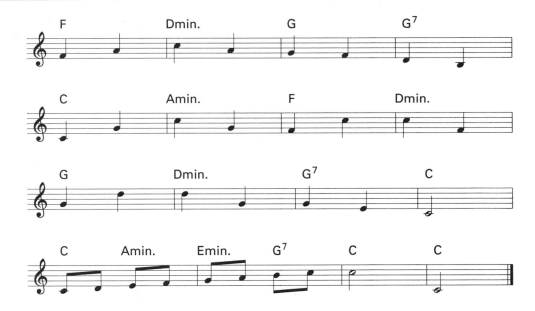

USING CHROMATIC PITCHES
TO CHANGE CHORD QUALITIES

The quality of any chord in a major or a minor key may be changed to add harmonic color to a composition or to create a stronger harmonic movement. This may be done by replacing one or more of the chord tones with a temporary chromatic pitch that is not found in the key. These changes of chord quality must add beauty to the composition and should not conflict with pitches in the melody. Three of the many chord-progression possibilities using changes in chord quality are notated in examples 12.10 through 12.12. Study and learn to perform these examples, then apply this principle to other chords within different progressions presented in this chapter. Listen closely as you apply this principle to change chord qualities and your ears will help you make good choices.

A. The minor vi chord may be chromatically altered to become a dominant VI^7 chord. This quality change creates a stronger harmonic movement to the ii chord.

12.10a C major: I vi^6 ii V$^6_5$ I

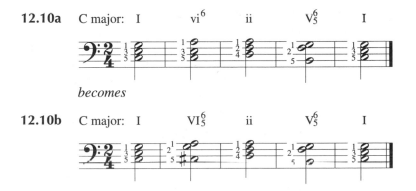

becomes

12.10b C major: I VI$^6_5$ ii V$^6_5$ I

B. The major I chord may be chromatically altered to become a I⁷ chord. This quality change creates a stronger harmonic movement to the IV chord.

becomes

C. The major quality of the IV chord in a major key may be temporarily changed to the minor quality of the iv chord from the parallel minor key to add harmonic color.

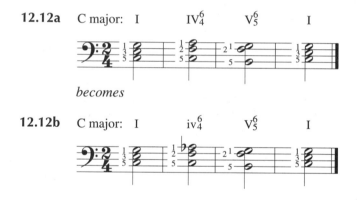

becomes

MODULATION

Many music compositions **modulate** (change keys) either temporarily or permanently. For example, a song may begin in the key of C major, modulate to the key of F major for harmonic variety, then return to the key of C major for its ending tonality. Modulation may also be used to heighten the feeling of climax in a longer work. For example, a piece may begin in the key of C major and move up through the keys of D and E major to end in the higher key of F major.

The Use of Common Chords and Secondary Dominant Chords for Harmonic Modulation

A harmonic modulation may be initiated by the use of a chord common to both keys. For example, in a modulation from C major to F major, the ii (D minor) chord in C major may be thought of as the vi chord (D minor) in F major. The composer, who began the piece in C major, thinks of the D minor chord as a vi chord in the key of F major and continues creating the piece in the new key. Study and perform the following example.

12.13

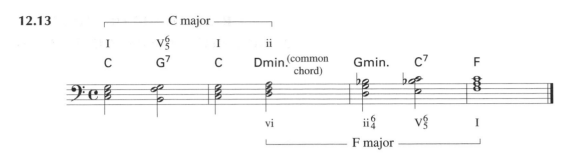

Another chord widely used to initiate a modulation is the **secondary dominant seventh,** a dominant seventh chord constructed on any scale degree other than the fifth. For example, in a modulation from C major to F major, the I⁷ (C dominant seventh) becomes the V⁷ (C dominant seventh) of the new key of F major. Study and perform the following example.

12.14

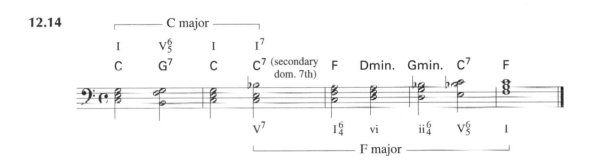

Direct Modulation

The most abrupt form of modulation occurs when a piece changes key without the use of a transitional harmony such as a common chord or a secondary dominant chord. The composer or performer simply moves to a new key by using a chord found only in the new tonality, thus creating a striking modulation. The degree of surprise the listener experiences will depend upon the new key chosen.

ASSIGNMENT

1. Practice performing the chord progressions introduced in this chapter in all major and minor keys.

2. Use the information presented in this chapter to create your own chord progressions in different major and minor keys.

3. Practice improvising melodies above the chord progressions you create.

4. Practice improvising chord progressions to accompany melodies that are familiar to you.

5. Create, notate, and perform for friends or classmates a major melody with a chord accompaniment that uses both primary and secondary chords.

ORIGINAL MELODY NO. 5
IN MAJOR WITH CHORD ACCOMPANIMENT

6. Create, notate, and perform for friends or classmates a minor melody with a chord accompaniment that uses both primary and secondary chords.

ORIGINAL MELODY NO. 6
IN MINOR WITH CHORD ACCOMPANIMENT

chapter 13

Chords, Chord Symbols, and Chord Progressions in Jazz and Popular Music

CHORD SYMBOLS IN JAZZ AND POPULAR MUSIC

Unfortunately, there is no standard method of writing the chord symbols used in jazz and popular music. A C major triad may be indicated by the symbols C, C MA, C maj., C△, and so on; and a C minor triad may be identified by the symbols C MI, C min., C–, and so on. In Table 14 (page 170), the most widely accepted symbols are presented along with the chords they represent. In addition, some of the less frequently used symbols appear in parentheses alongside the preferred symbols.

Chord symbols in jazz and popular music do not show the chord's relationship to a key as does the numeral system of chord identification presented in Chapter 10. Instead these chord symbols indicate the root of the chord with a capital letter (C, D, etc.), and additional parts of the symbol (MA, ♯, ⁷, etc.) indicate the structure of the chord. Most often the structure is achieved by piling up intervals of a third one on top of the other above the chord's root. The exceptions to chord structure by thirds occur when a major sixth is added above the root, when a perfect fourth replaces the third of a suspended chord, and when the arabic numeral 4 indicates a chord constructed by piling up perfect fourths above the root. Only one of the chord symbols represents a chord inversion; pitches intended to be played in the bass are identified by a letter appearing below a diagonal line. For example, C/G indicates a C major triad with a G (fifth of chord) in the bass.

CONSTRUCTION OF CHORDS IN JAZZ AND POPULAR MUSIC

To create jazz-style harmonies, triads and dominant seventh chords *must* be extended. Triads are extended to become major or minor sixth chords, major or minor seventh chords, or major or minor ninth chords. Dominant seventh chords are extended to ninth, eleventh, or thirteenth chords, and often they have altered chord tones such as flatted or sharped ninths or fifths. Although popular music includes the wide use of triads and dominant seventh chords, extended jazz chords are also an important part of the harmonic vocabulary of this style of music.

Study and perform the following extended chords. The C major and C minor triads are extended to sixth, seventh, and ninth chords. The C dominant seventh chord is extended to ninth, eleventh, and thirteenth chords. Notice that a chord may be extended only to a thirteenth chord; any further extension of the thirteenth chord only doubles one of the seven pitches that make up this chord.

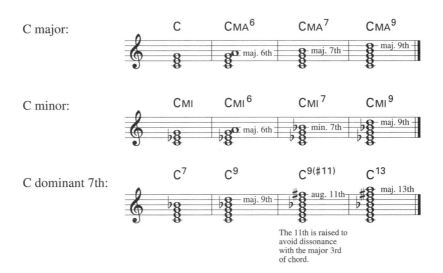

See Table 14 (page 170) for additional jazz-style chords and their symbols.

CHORDS AND RELATED SCALES

Because jazz and popular music make frequent use of harmonies that are outside the basic tonality of the composition, musicians often use many different scales within the same piece when composing or improvising melodies. Table 15 (page 171) identifies a few of the many scales that may be played with chords that are used frequently in jazz and popular harmonies. The explanation and notation of these scales may be found in Chapter 6. Perform each chord and a related scale simultaneously, and listen to how well the chord and its related scales sound together. *Memorize* those sounds.

COMMON CHORD PROGRESSIONS
AND KEYBOARD VOICINGS

All of the chord progressions and information related to chord progressions, chord substitutions, modulations, and harmonization of melodies presented in Chapter 12 also apply to music performed in the jazz or popular styles. The two main differences are the use of extended chords (sevenths, ninths, elevenths, and thirteenths) and the use of dominant-type chords not only in the traditional function of moving to the tonic chord (V7–I) but also as harmonic entities in their own right without the arbitrary sense of resolution to the tonic chord.

Study and learn to play on a keyboard instrument the major and minor chord progressions on pages 171–173. Exercises 13.1–13.4 use what is perhaps the most common chord progression in tonal music (major: I–vi–ii–V–I; minor: i–♯vi°–ii°–V–i), and exercises 13.5 and 13.6 use common "blues" progressions.

Because four pitches are required to achieve the unique sound of each extended chord, use both the left and the right hands. With your left hand, play the root of each chord; with your right hand, play one of two basic **chord voicings** (arrangement of

TABLE 14   Chord Symbols and Chord Construction

Chord constructed with perf. 4ths above root.

C dom. 7th, Bb (7th) in bass.

Polychord symbol: two chords played simultaneously, A maj. triad played above a Bb maj. triad.

chord tones above a bass note). The first voicing can be identified as the *voicing of the seventh*; it places the seventh of the chord above the bass note. Three voicings of the seventh will be used, and they include the following additional tones above the root: R/7-3-5, R/7-3-13 (the thirteenth is the same as the enharmonic sixth), and R/7-9-3 (the ninth is the same as the enharmonic second). The second voicing can be identified as the *voicing of the third*; it places the third of the chord above the bass note. Two voicings of the third will be used, and they include the following additional tones above the root: R/3-5-7 and R/3-7-9. Notice that the chord voicing of the seventh and the chord voicing of the third alternate in the following chord progressions. The exceptions in the alternation of these voicings are as follows: the second measure in example 13.4, where a R/b5-7-3 voicing is used for a smoother voice leading, and measure 10 of example 13.6, where the voicing does not change.

TABLE 15   Chords and Related Scales

Chord	Related scale
Major 7th	Major, Lydian*
Major 6th, or 6/9	Major pentatonic*
Minor 7th (i function)	Natural minor (Aeolian), Dorian,* Minor pentatonic,* Blues
Minor 7th (ii function)	Dorian,* Minor pentatonic,* Blues
Minor 7th (iii or vi function)	Natural minor (Aeolian), Phrygian
Minor 6th, or 6/9	Dorian,* Melodic minor,* Minor pentatonic,* Blues
Dominant 7th, 9th, 13th (unaltered)	Mixolydian, Major pentatonic*
Dominant 7th (♭5) or (♯5)	Whole-tone*
Dominant 7th (♭9)	Half-step–whole-step diminished,* 5th mode of harmonic minor (same as harmonic minor scale constructed on the pitch a perfect 5th below the root of the dominant 7th chord)
Dominant 7th (♯9)	Half-step–whole-step diminished,* Blues, Minor pentatonic, Dorian
Dominant 7th sus	Mixolydian, Minor pentatonic scale constructed on the 5th of the dominant 7th chord*
Minor 7th (♭5)	Locrian, 2nd mode of harmonic minor (same as harmonic minor scale constructed on the pitch a major second below the root of the minor 7th (♭5) chord)
Diminished 7th	Whole-step–half-step diminished

*These scales have no dissonant ("wrong") pitches.

13.1   Learn to play this chord progression in C major. Then transpose it and learn to play it in all major keys.[1]

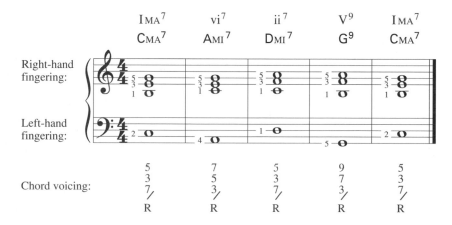

[1]See Appendix I for suggested guitar voicings for chord progressions 13.1–13.6, and see Appendix J for suggested rhythms to use while playing these chord progressions.

13.2   Learn to play this chord progression in C major. Then transpose it and learn to play it in all major keys.

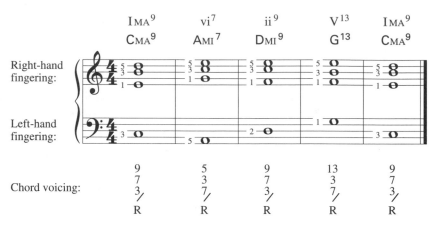

13.3   Learn to play this chord progression in C minor. Then transpose it and learn to play it in all minor keys.

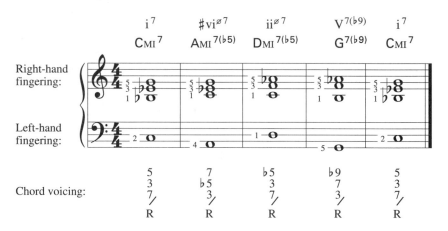

13.4   Learn to play this chord progression in C minor. Then transpose it and learn to play it in all minor keys.

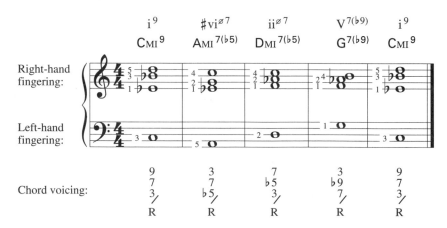

13.5   Learn to play this "blues" chord progression in C major. Then transpose it and learn to play it in all major keys.

*These chords are played only when repeating this blues progression.

13.6   Learn to play this "blues" chord progression in C minor. Then transpose it and learn to play it in all minor keys.

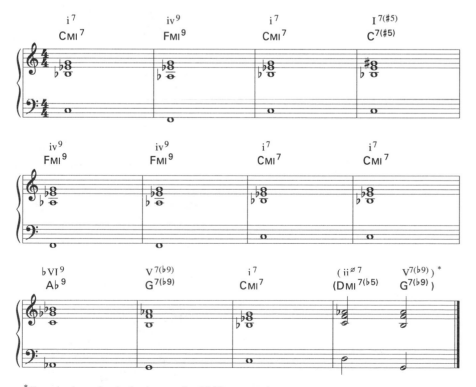

*These chords are played only when repeating this blues progression.

After you have learned to play exercises 13.1–13.6, apply these basic voicings, which use extended chords, to the chord progressions presented in Chapter 12. Finally, apply them to jazz and popular songs you wish to perform. When using the basic voicings of the seventh and the third, keep the following suggestions in mind to help you choose between them.

1. When the root moves by a fifth (fourth), change the voicing.

CMA⁷	to	FMA⁷		CMA⁷	to	FMA⁷
a. R/7-3-5		R/3-7-9		**b.** R/3-7-9		R/7-3-5

2. When the root moves by a third, either change the voicing or keep the same voicing.

CMA⁷	to	AMI⁷	*or*	CMA⁷	to	AMI⁷
a. R/7-3-5		R/3-5-7		R/7-3-5		R/7-3-5
b. R/3-7-9		R/7-3-5		R/3-7-9		R/3-7-9

3. When the root moves by a second, keep the same voicing.

CMA⁷	to	DMI⁷		CMA⁷	to	DMI⁷
a. R/7-3-5		R/7-3-5		**b.** R/3-7-9		R/3-7-9

Study, listen to, and learn to perform *Just Sing It!* (example 13.7). Compare this version, which harmonizes the melody with extended jazz-style chords, with versions 1.1 (page 2) and 12.9 (page 162).

 13.7

DIATONIC AND CHROMATIC HARMONIC SUBSTITUTIONS AND CHORD EMBELLISHMENTS

The following chord substitutions include the substitutions introduced in Chapter 12, but they are presented as they function with extended jazz-style chords. In addition, new substitutions commonly used in jazz and popular music are presented. Keep in mind that substitute chords must work well with the melody. For example, a $G^{7(\flat 9)}$ would not substitute for a G^7 if the melody contained an A-natural; the $A\flat$ ($\flat 9$) would create an unacceptable dissonance with the A-natural.

A. iii^7 (EMI^7) substitutes for IMA^7 (CMA^7), good when moving to vi^7 (AMI^7).

B. vi^7 (AMI^7) substitutes for IMA^7 (CMA^7), good when moving to ii^7 (DMI^7).

C. Chord substitutions may be borrowed from parallel minor or major keys.

For example: IMA^7 (CMA^7) to ii^7 (DMI^7) may use the substitution
IMA^7 (CMA^7) to ii$^{\varnothing 7}$ (DMI$^{7(\flat 5)}$) (ii$^{\varnothing 7}$ from parallel minor)

IMA^7 (CMA^7) to IVMA^7 (FMA^7) may use the substitution
IMA^7 (CMA^7) to iv^7 (FMI^7) (iv^7 from parallel minor)

D. Secondary dominant sevenths may be substituted for other chord qualities.

For example: vi^7 (AMI^7) becomes VI^7 (A^7)

IMA^7 (CMA^7) or i^7 (CMI^7) becomes I^7 (C^7)

E. Altered dominant sevenths may be substituted for unaltered dominant chords.

For example: V^7 (G^7) becomes V$^{7(\flat 9)}$ (G$^{7(\flat 9)}$) (V$^{7(\flat 9)}$ from parallel minor)

$$
\text{Additional alterations:} \quad V^7 \left\{ \begin{array}{l} \flat 9 \\ \sharp 9 \\ \sharp 5 \text{ or } \flat 13 \\ \flat 5 \text{ or } \sharp 11 \end{array} \right.
$$

F. Secondary diminished sevenths chords that move chromatically may be used to connect two diatonic chords.

For example:

IMA^7	$\sharp$i$^{\circ 7}$	ii^7
CMA^7	C$\sharp^\circ$	DMI^7

ii^7	$\sharp$ii$^{\circ 7}$	iii^7
DMI^7	D$\sharp^\circ$	EMI^7

iii^7	$\flat$iii$^{\circ 7}$	ii^7
EMI^7	E$\flat^\circ$	DMI^7

G. Secondary ii–V^7–I progressions may be inserted into original chord progressions. Any chord may be preceded with the insertion of its ii–V^7 or just its V^7.

For example:

CMA^7	DMI^7	G^7	CMA^7
/ / / /	/ / / /	/ / / /	/ / / /

becomes:

CMA^7	EMI^7 A^7	DMI^7 G^7	CMA^7
/ / / /	/ / / /	/ / / /	/ / / /

H. Substitute a diminished seventh chord for a dominant seventh chord. Construct the diminished seventh chord on the third of the dominant seventh chord.

For example: G^7 becomes B$^\circ$

I. The **tritone substitution** substitutes a dominant seventh chord whose root is a tritone above the root of the original dominant seventh; Db^7 substitutes for G^7.

For example: IMA^7 V^9 IMA^7
                CMA^7 G^9 CMA^7
                / / / / | / / / / | / / / /   ‖

becomes: IMA^7 bII^{13} IMA^7
            CMA^7 Db^{13} CMA^7
            / / / / | / / / / | / / / /   ‖

An extension of the tritone substitution is called the diminished cycle. The **diminished cycle** is the substitution of a dominant seventh chord with another dominant seventh chord whose root is one of the tones of a diminished seventh chord constructed on the root of the original dominant seventh. Study the following three sets of dominant seventh chords that substitute for one another. Notice that the pitches of each set form a diminished seventh chord and that any of the four tones may serve as the root of the dominant substitution. These three sets include all twelve substitution possibilities.

1. C^7, Eb^7, Gb^7, A^7 (All four of these chords substitute for one another.)

2. $C\#^7$, E^7, G^7, Bb^7 (All four of these chords substitute for one another.)

3. D^7, F^7, Ab^7, B^7 (All four of these chords substitute for one another.)

J. Chord qualities may be substituted.

For example: Major chords may become dominant chords; IMA^7 becomes I^7.

Minor chords may become dominant chords; ii^7 becomes II^7.

Dominant chords may become major or minor chords; V^7 becomes VMA^7 or v^7.

K. Substitute $ii–V^7$ a half step above original $ii–V^7$. This is a form of sideslipping to create dissonance.

For example: DMI^7 G^7 CMA^7
                / / / / | / / / / | / / / /   ‖

becomes: $EbMI^7$ Ab^7 DMI^7 G^7 CMA^7
            / / / / | / / / / | / / / /   ‖

CREATING HARMONIES FROM MODES

Much jazz and popular music is created using modes rather than major or minor scales. These modal compositions derive their harmonies in ways unrelated to the major/ minor tonal system. The dorian mode is one of the most widely used modes, and nearly anything is harmonically possible if the bass line remains centered on the root of the mode (D in D dorian, G in G dorian, etc.).

Chords are created by combining various scale degrees (three or more) in numerous combinations and inversions. There is no consistent approach to chord construction, the progression of chords, or the symbolizing of modal harmonies. Study and perform the following examples.

In diatonic **planing** (parallel motion), second-inversion triads created from the pitches of a given mode are often played above the root of the mode. For example, random second-inversion triads from the D dorian mode may be played above a D **pedal tone** (sustained tone).

Diatonic planing

D pedal tone

Chromatically altered second-inversion triads may be added to the planing technique in a given mode. For example, random second-inversion triads that include chromatically altered triads from the D dorian mode may be played above a D pedal tone.

Chromatic planing

D pedal tone

Random planing of different diatonic chord types and voicings extracted from a given mode may be played above the root of a given mode; and random planing of different chromatic chord types above a pedal tone without regard to mode, chord qualities, or voicings may also be used. For example, the following chord sequences include a mixture of chord types played in a variety of voicings that include quartal voicings.

Random diatonic planing   Random chromatic planing

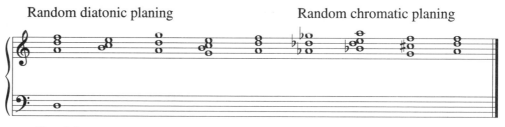

D pedal tone

Chords that are not too distant from the fundamental mode should be sounded occasionally to reinforce the mode of the composition. The use of the I, IV, and V chords from the parent major scale also helps to establish the sound of the fundamental mode. For example, in D dorian, C (I), F (IV), and G (V) chords are from the parent key, C major.

ASSIGNMENT

Create, notate, and perform for friends or classmates a jazz- or popular-style melody with chord accompaniment. Use extended jazz-style chords to harmonize your melody, and notate the chords with symbols written above the notated melody.

ORIGINAL MELODY NO. 7
WITH JAZZ-STYLE HARMONIES

chapter **14**

Composing a Song

WHERE TO BEGIN

A **song** is a short musical composition for voice written to express a text. The song may be a melody with lyrics performed unaccompanied, or it may be accompanied by additional music written for solo instruments such as the piano or the guitar, or ensembles such as a choir or an orchestra.

There are as many valid approaches to composing a song as there are songwriters. Some composers begin by writing their own lyrics or choosing a poem written by another person; then they create music that appropriately expresses the text. This approach was used by the great nineteenth-century composer Franz Schubert, who took poems by Johann Goethe and set them to music. Other composers create melodies first, then write lyrics that work well with the pitches, rhythms, and emotional expression of their melody, or choose a lyricist to write an appropriate text for their song. The famous twentieth-century composer George Gershwin used this approach. He wrote beautiful harmonized melodies; then his brother, Ira, wrote the lyrics to complete the song. Although many songwriters prefer one way or the other, many composers write well using either approach.

Which approach to use is a choice that you the composer must make. If an idea for lyrics comes to you first, you will want to work from the lyrics; if a melodic or harmonic idea comes to you first, you will want to work from the music. Remember, however, that when you write the music for existing lyrics, the lyrics must be used to guide your choice of style, meter, tonality, and form. Likewise, if you are writing lyrics for an existing melody, the subject, emotion, and form of your lyrics will be dictated by the music.

As you gain experience, you will find that once you begin composing, your initial idea will lead you step-by-step through a creative process that will seem more intuitive than planned. The lyrics may suggest a rhythmic idea that becomes a melody, which then suggests a chord progression; or a chord progression may suggest a melody that in turn suggests the lyrics. Occasionally all the elements of a song seem to come to the composer simultaneously. A central idea—the subject for the lyrics, a chord progression, or a melodic or rhythmic idea—will spark a burst of creative activity from which the lyrics, melody, and harmonization seem to evolve at the same time. When that happens, notate your song quickly, without questioning its quality. You can make improvements later if necessary.

A SIX-STEP APPROACH TO SONGWRITING

As already stated, you will eventually write songs less and less by method and more and more by intuition. However, to begin developing your songwriting skills, you may want to use the following six-step approach.

1. *Lyrics:* Create original lyrics, or borrow a text from a preexisting source. Choose an interesting subject that you feel will lend itself well to a melodic treatment. The lyrics may be in the form either of a short poem with a set meter for each **verse**[1] or of a short prose statement without a set meter or rhyme. Following are two examples of texts that are suitable for song lyrics. Lyric A is a poem that was generated from the thought that a person must "reach out" to find love; lyric B is a prose statement expressing the thought that loneliness can be experienced even in a crowded society unless an effort is made to make friends. The creation of both lyrics began as verbal improvisations. Then, with some rethinking and written revisions, they arrived at their present form. If you find writing the lyrics for an original song to be difficult, then use a borrowed text, a favorite poem, or a statement written by someone else. If you use another person's text, you must remember to give proper credit, and if the material is copyrighted, you must get permission to use it.

   Lyric A

   Reach out, reach out, and find true love.
   Reach out, reach out, and experience the unknown.
   Reach out for someone, let your heart wander freely.
   You must reach out or your soul walks alone.

   Risk it all, the chance is worth taking.
   Risk it all, . . .

   Lyric B

   Yesterday as I walked a crowded street, a lonely feeling came over me.
   Here I am among all these people, friendless and alone.
   Are the people I pass feeling as I do? Are they alone, . . .

2. *Rhythm and Meter:* After you have written out your lyrics, decide upon a tempo and a rhythmic style that will help express the words you are setting to music. Then while tapping the basic beat, begin to recite the lyrics in a rhythmic manner dictated by the syllables of each word and your personal choice. Although each syllable will receive a rhythmic value, the length of the rhythm is up to you. In addition, more than one rhythm (note) may be set to a syllable. Because each of the lyrics have many rhythm possibilities, experiment with different rhythms before you decide which is most appropriate.

   When you have decided on the rhythm you are going to use for your song, notate it above the lyrics as shown in the following examples. Then recite the lyrics in rhythm and establish where the meter accents fall. This process will help you identify the meter of your song.

---

[1] A verse, also called a **stanza,** is a group of lines in a poem or in the lyrics of a song.

Study and recite the following examples.

Lyric A, Rhythm 1

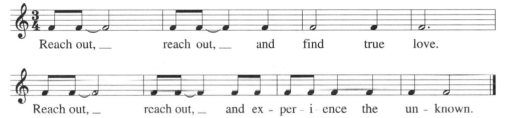

Lyric A, Rhythm 2

Lyric B, Rhythm 1

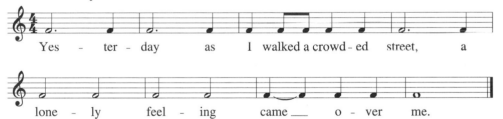

Lyric B, Rhythm 2

3. *Tonality and Melody:* Ask yourself, "Will my lyrics be expressed best by a melody in a major or a minor key?" Then play a major scale on the piano in a range that you can sing comfortably. Next, play the parallel minor scale and decide which scale, major or minor, will provide the pitch material that best expresses the message of your lyrics.

After you have established the key for your song, begin using pitches from the scale you have chosen to improvise a melody that expresses your lyrics. You may sing your improvised melody or play it on the piano. As you improvise, use the rhythms and the meter you created by following step 2.

Remember, there are many melodic (pitch) possibilities that will fit your lyrics and the rhythms you have created. Improvise many different melodies, building from one phrase into the next; as you develop your melody, feel free to change rhythms or lyrics you created earlier if it will improve your song. As you improvise, look for words that suggest high or low pitches, smooth or disjunct melodic movement, repeated pitches, melodic repetition, or sequences. Keep trying different melodic ideas for each phrase of the text until you find the melody that you feel expresses the lyrics.

Study and perform the following melodic examples. These examples combine the opening lines of lyric A and lyric B with rhythm possibilities A1, A2, and B1, B2. Notice that each of the lyrics has two melodic settings in a major key and two melodic settings in the parallel minor key. Each melody, therefore, expresses the lyrics in a slightly different way. Which melody do you feel most faithfully expresses each of the lyrics?

Lyric A, Rhythm 1, C major Melody

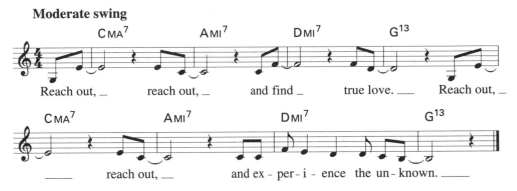

Lyric A, Rhythm 1, C minor Melody

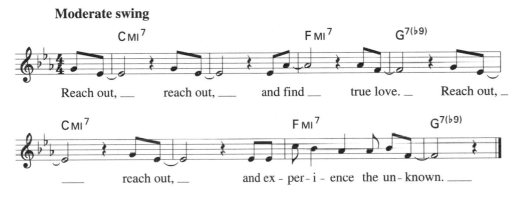

Lyric A, Rhythm 2, C major Melody

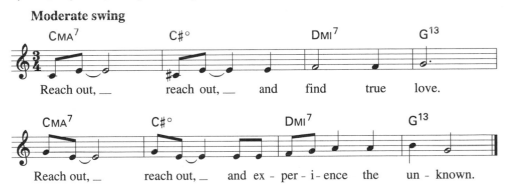

Lyric A, Rhythm 2, C minor Melody

Lyric B, Rhythm 1, C major Melody

Lyric B, Rhythm 1, C minor Melody

Lyric B, Rhythm 2, C major Melody

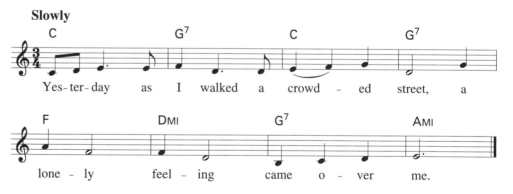

Lyric B, Rhythm 2, C minor Melody

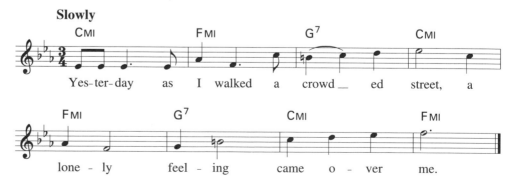

4. *Form:* The form of your song will be dictated by the lyrics and your choice to use or not use repeated melodic material. If the text does not lend itself to the use of repeated melodic material (each of the several phrases suggesting new melodic ideas), your song will develop into a through-composed form. A melody in **through-composed form** is nonsectional; it has no repeated phrases or sections. Each line of the text is set to new music. Study and learn to perform *Scarborough Fair,* notated below.

Scarborough Fair is in through-composed form in that it is nonsectional, devoid of repeated phrases. This song, however, has several verses; therefore, different lyrics are sung to the same melody as the song is repeated. When a song sets several verses to the same music, it is called **strophic.** Because *Scarborough Fair* is strophic, it could be thought of as a modified through-composed form. Schubert's *Erlking* (listed at the end of this chapter) is a true through-composed song because each line of the entire text is set to new music.

SCARBOROUGH FAIR

2. Tell her to make me a cambric shirt,
   Parsley, sage, rosemary and thyme.
   Without no seams nor needle work,
   Then she'll be a true love of mine.

3. Tell her to find me an acre of land,
   Parsley, sage, rosemary and thyme.
   Between the salt water and the sea strands,
   Then she'll be a true love of mine.

If your lyrics fall into distinct sections that may be set to the same or different melodic material, your song may fit nicely into a two-part or a three-part form. A piece in **two-part form** has two contrasting sections of music, and when referred to analytically they are labeled for identification with the letters A and B (A section, B section). Pieces in **three-part form** have three sections of music: an A section, a contrasting B section, and the return of the A section. Because these forms are widely used for composing songs, they are sometimes referred to as **two-part song form** and **three-part song form.** Although the A and B sections contain contrasting materials, melodic repetition may or may not exist within each section.

Study the possibilities of the two- and three-part song forms suggested below. Then study and learn to perform *Water Come to Me Eye* and *Rock-A My Soul.*

Two-part form	**Three-part form**
A B	A B A
A A B	A A B A
A B B	A B A A
A A B B	A B B A

Water Come to Me Eye is in two-part form. The first two phrases form the A section, and the third and fourth phrases form the B section. This song is strophic, for it is usually sung with slight changes in the lyrics of the A section as the song is repeated. The B section of this two-part song is a **chorus,**[2] so the same lyrics are sung for the B section each time the melody is repeated.

WATER COME TO ME EYE

---

[2]A chorus, also called a **refrain,** is a phrase repeated after each verse (stanza).

Rock-A My Soul is in three-part form: A section (eight measures), B section (eight measures), and the repeat (*D.C. al Fine*) of the A section.

ROCK-A MY SOUL

5. *Notation:* As you create the melody for your song, you will need to notate each phrase as you improvise it, then erase and notate corrections as you try different ideas and make slight changes. After you have finished composing your melody, notate your song as neatly as possible. Be careful to space your notation so the lyrics may be written with each syllable placed below its corresponding melody note. Study the song examples in this lesson to help guide your notation efforts.

6. *Harmonization:* After you have written the melody of your song create a harmonization for it. Use chords and chord progressions appropriate for the style of your piece.

STUDY GREAT SONGS

There are many great songs written in all musical styles. Listed on the next page are just a few outstanding songwriters and some of the great songs they have written. Listen to recordings of these songs. Then learn to perform them, for studying the lyrics, melodies, and chord progressions of great songs will help you become a better songwriter.

The art of songwriting goes back as far as the history of music, and the pleasures experienced by both professional and amateur composers keep this art alive in all cultures around the world. Now it is time for you to join this family of creative musicians. You can do it! Take action!

Composer	Lyricist	Song title
Franz Schubert	J. Goethe	*The Erlking*
	J. Goethe	*Gretchen at the Spinning Wheel*
George Gershwin	I. Gershwin	*Our Love Is Here to Stay*
	I. Gershwin/Heyward	*Summertime*
	I. Gershwin	*They Can't Take That Away from Me*
Cole Porter		*All of You*
		Night and Day
		What Is This Thing Called Love?
Hoagy Carmichael	S. Gorrell	*Georgia on My Mind*
	M. Parish	*Stardust*
Antonio Carlos Jobim		*Corcovado (Quiet Nights)*
	DeMoraes/Gimbel	*Girl from Ipanema*
Jerome Kern	O. Hammerstein	*All the Things You Are*
	J. Mercer	*Dearly Beloved*
	O. Hammerstein	*The Song Is You*
Erroll Garner	J. Burke	*Misty*
Elton John	B. Taupin	*Daniel*
John Lennon & Paul McCartney		*Eleanor Rigby*
		Fool on the Hill
		Michelle
Kenny Loggins		*Danny's Song*
		House at Pooh Corner
Bob Wills		*San Antonio Rose*
Marty Robbins		*El Paso*
Willie Nelson		*Crazy*
James Taylor		*Country Road*
		Fire and Rain
		Sweet Baby James
Paul Simon		*Bridge over Troubled Water*
		Homeward Bound
		Mrs. Robinson
Carole King		*You've Got a Friend*

ASSIGNMENT

Create, notate, and perform for friends or classmates an original harmonized song in either two-part, three-part, or through-composed form. Use the information provided in this lesson and previous lessons to guide you as you create your song.

ORIGINAL SONG

appendix A

Ear-Training Exercises—Rhythm

- Learn to hear notated rhythms by playing, singing, and *memorizing* the following rhythm patterns.
- Perform these exercises at slow, moderate, and fast tempos while using a metronome to tap a steady beat.
- Sing "la," and play G above middle C on the piano.

9.
10.
11.
12.
13.
14.
15.
16.
17.
18.
19.
(set metronome to beat eighth notes)
20.

appendix **B**

Ear-Training Exercises— Pitch

- The pitch sequences of melodies are made up of scale and chord patterns.
- Learn to hear notated melodies by playing, singing, and *memorizing* the following pitch patterns.
- Perform these exercises at slow, moderate, and fast tempos while using a metronome to tap a steady beat.

1. Scale/Chord Drills. See pages 85–87, drills A–E. Perform the drills in both major and minor keys.

2. C major triad (transpose and perform with chord root on all twelve pitches— B major, B♭ major, etc.).

3. C minor triad (transpose and perform with chord root on all twelve pitches— B minor, B♭ minor, etc.).

4. C diminished triad (transpose and perform with chord root on all twelve pitches—B dim., B♭ dim., etc.).

a.

root   3rd   5th

b.

root   3rd   5th

5. C augmented triad (transpose and perform with chord root on all twelve pitches—B aug., B♭ aug., etc.).

a.

root   3rd   5th

b.

root   3rd   5th

6. C major seventh chord (transpose and perform with chord root on all twelve pitches—B maj.⁷, B♭ maj.⁷, etc.).

a.

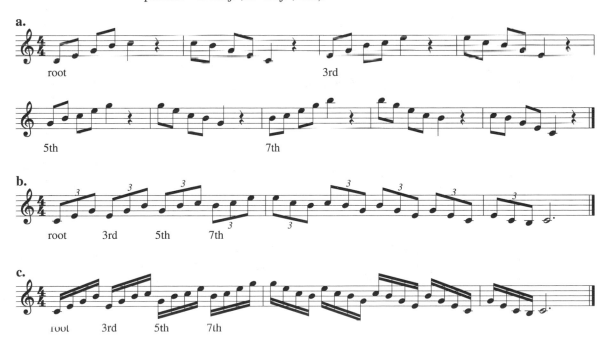

root   3rd

5th   7th

b.

root   3rd   5th   7th

c.

root   3rd   5th   7th

7. C dominant seventh chord (transpose and perform with chord root on all twelve pitches—B dom.⁷, B♭ dom.⁷, etc.).

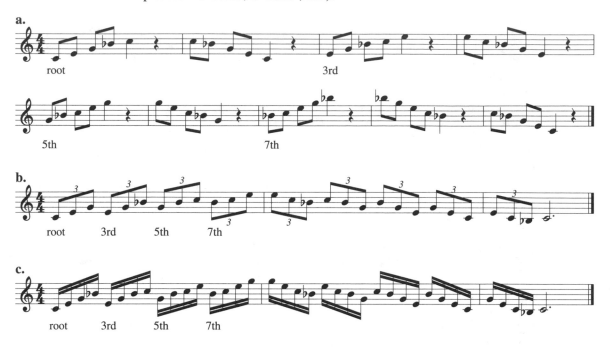

8. C minor seventh chord (transpose and perform with chord root on all twelve pitches—B min.⁷, B♭ min.⁷, etc.).

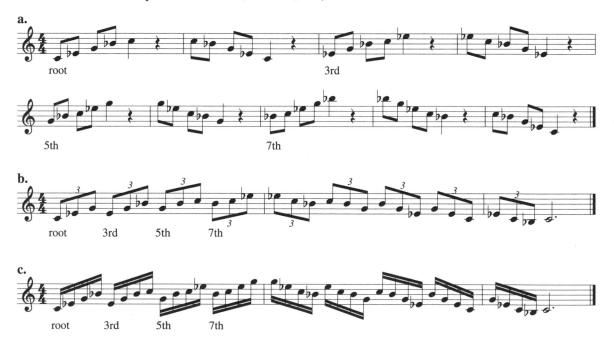

9. C half-diminished seventh chord (transpose and perform with chord root on all twelve pitches—B$^{\varnothing 7}$, B$\flat^{\varnothing 7}$, etc.).

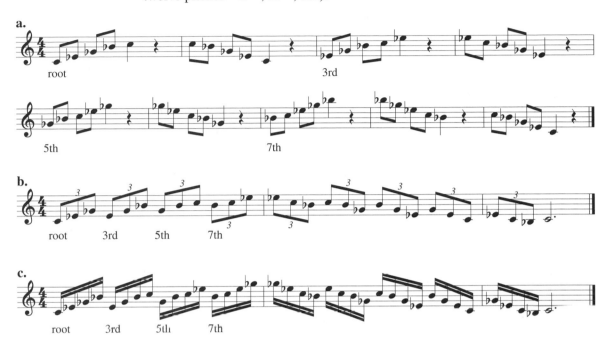

10. C diminished seventh chord (transpose and perform with chord root on all twelve pitches—B$^{\circ 7}$, B$\flat^{\circ 7}$, etc.).

11. See Aural Melodic Interval Drills 9.10, 9.11, and 9.12.

12. See Aural Harmonic Interval Drills 9.17, 9.18, and 9.19.

13. See Aural Triad Drills 10.9–10.15.

14. See Identifying the Dominant Seventh Chord by Sound, 10.18.

appendix C

Rhythm Studies

- Perform these exercises at slow, moderate, and fast tempos while using a metronome to tap a steady beat.
- Sing "la," and play G above middle C on the piano.
- Learn to perform the basic beat with the left hand on the pitch middle C as you sing and play these studies on the pitch G above middle C.
- Bracketed exercises may be performed simultaneously on the piano to create two-part rhythmic pieces. Play one part on middle C with the left hand; play the other part on G above middle C with the right hand.

11.
12.
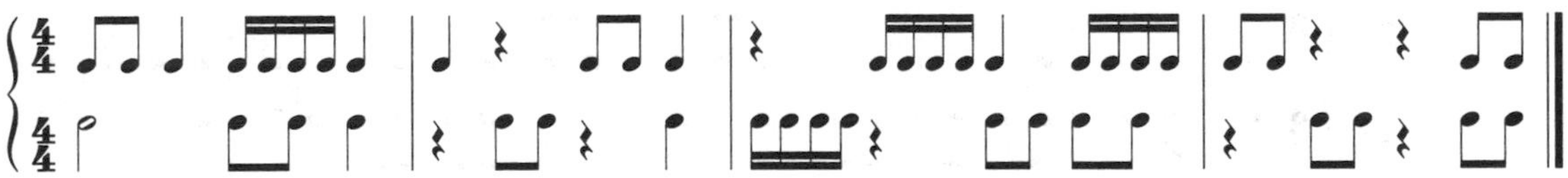

13.
14.
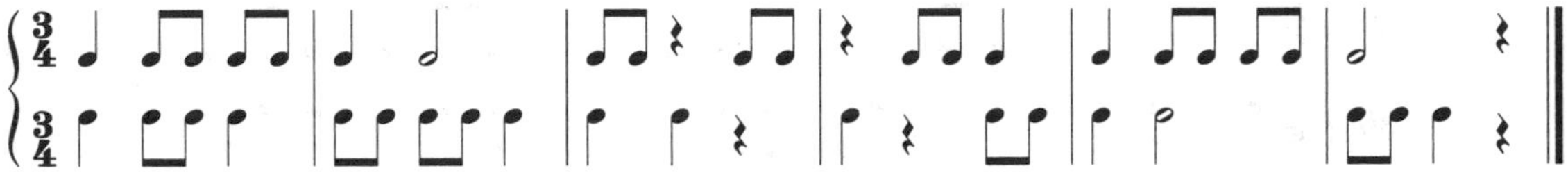

15.
16.
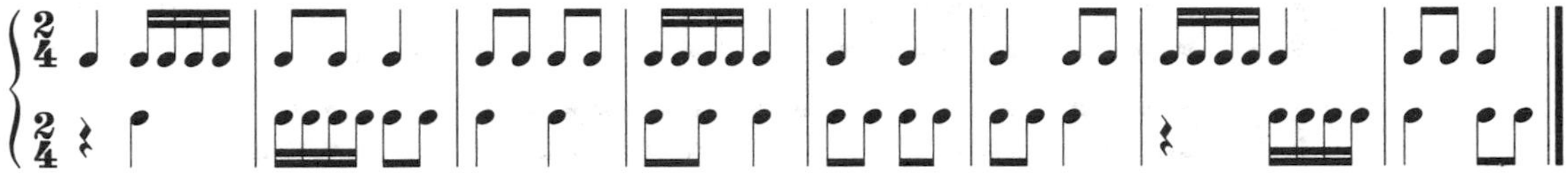

17.
18.
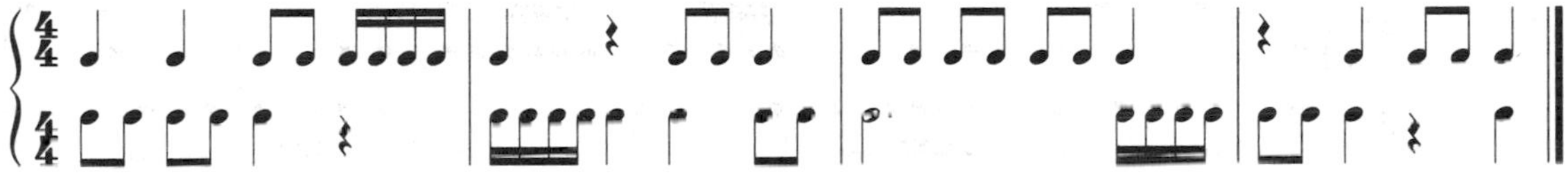

19.
20.
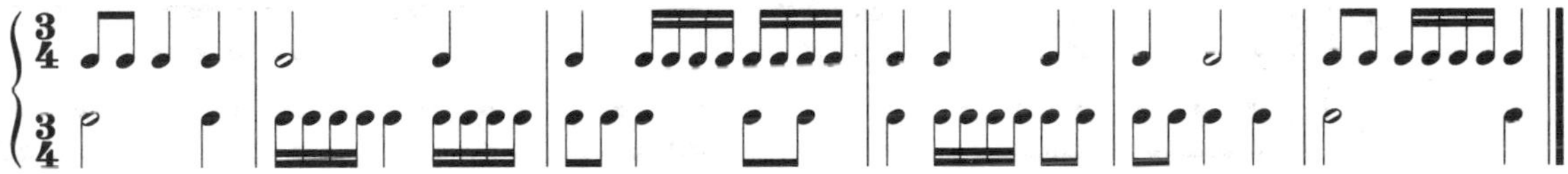

21.
22.
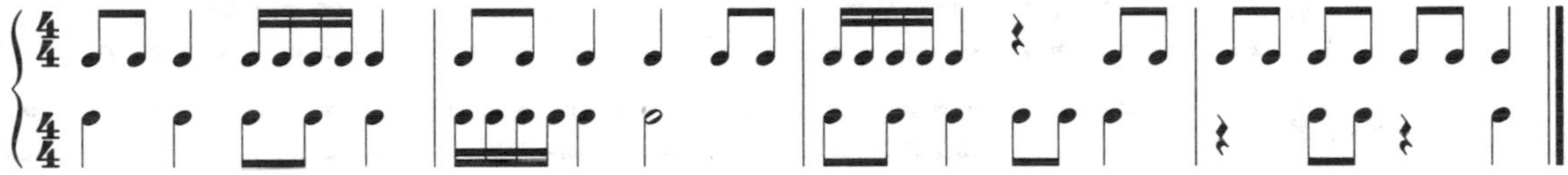

23.
24.
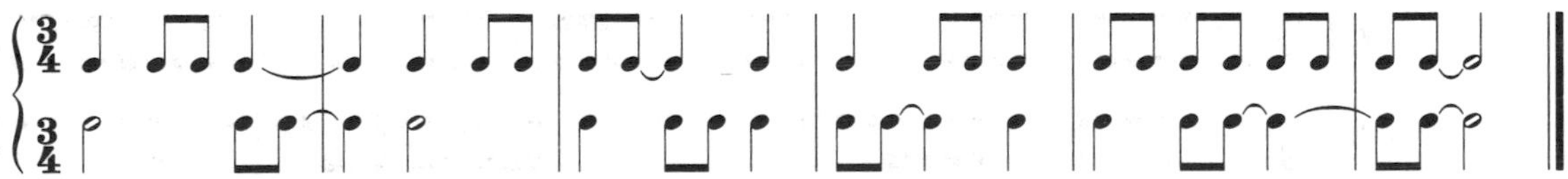

25.
26.
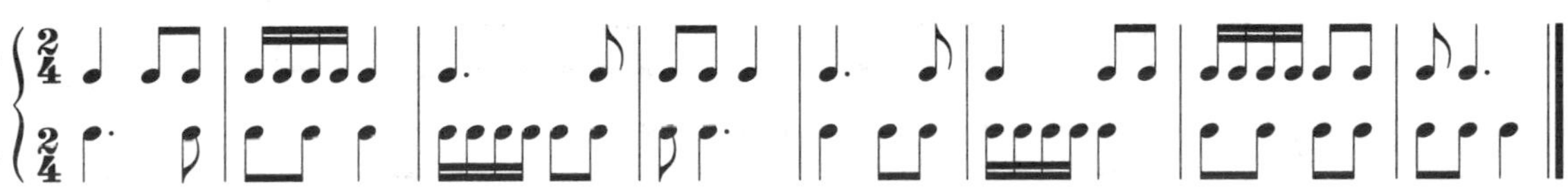

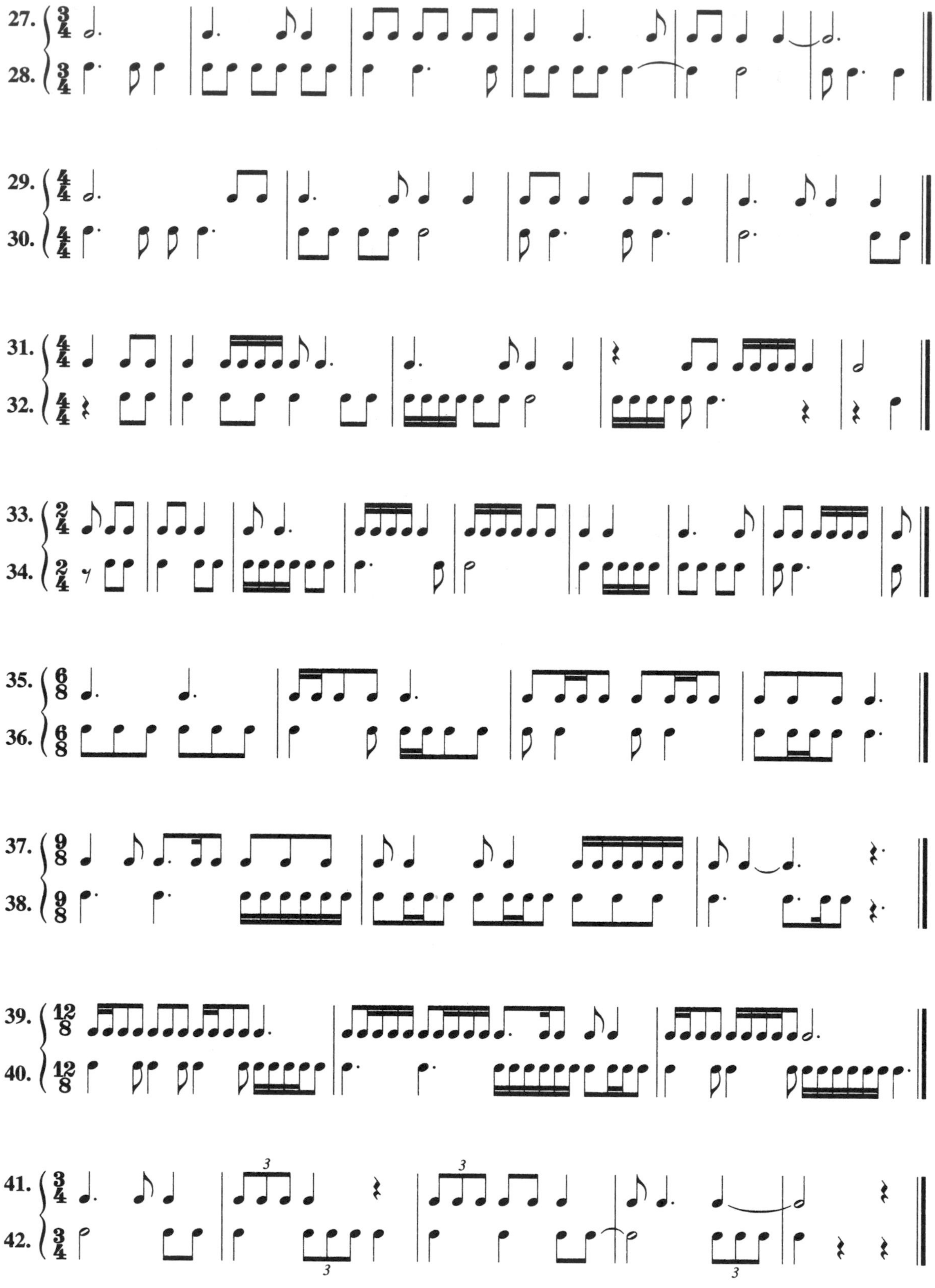
27.
28.
29.
30.
31.
32.
33.
34.
35.
36.
37.
38.
39.
40.
41.
42.

43.
44.
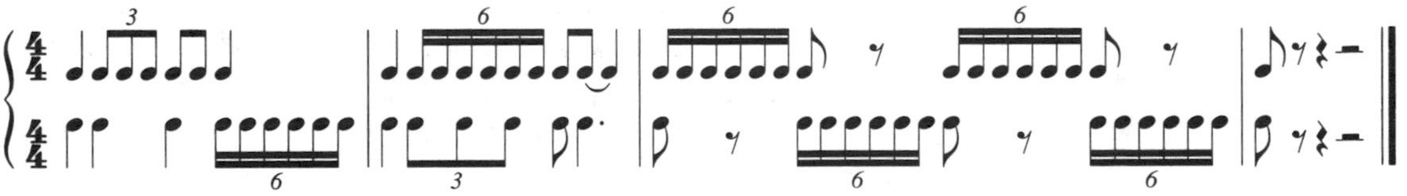

45.
46.
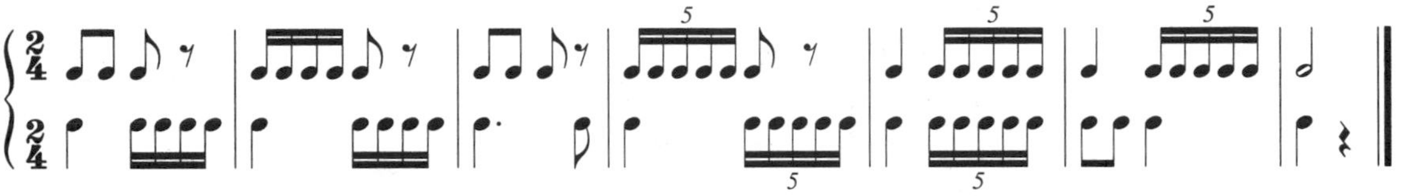

47.
48.
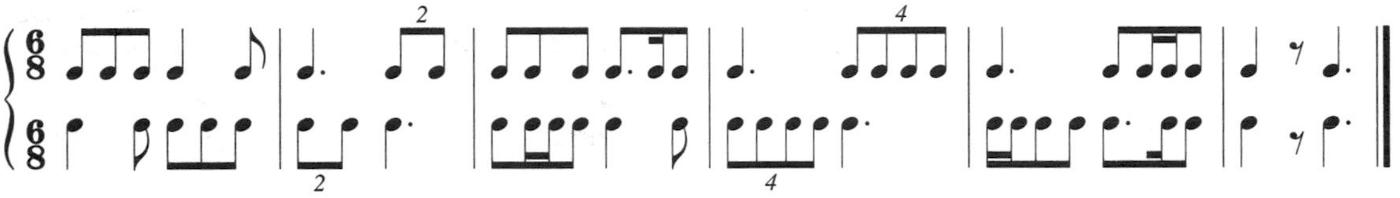

49.
50.
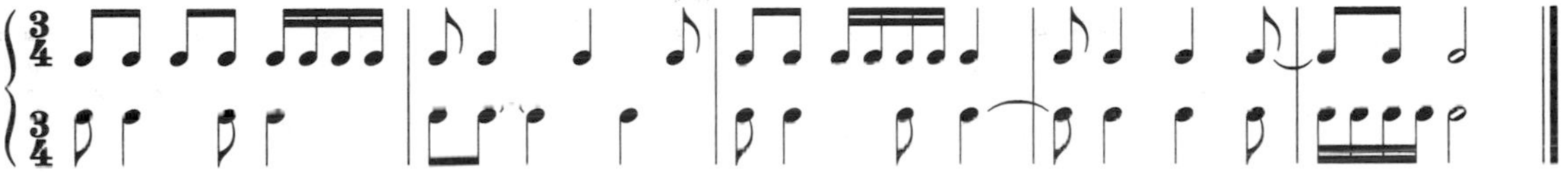

51.
52.
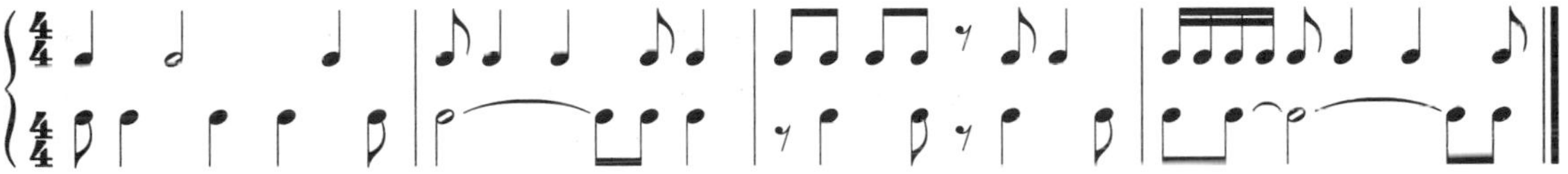

53.
54.
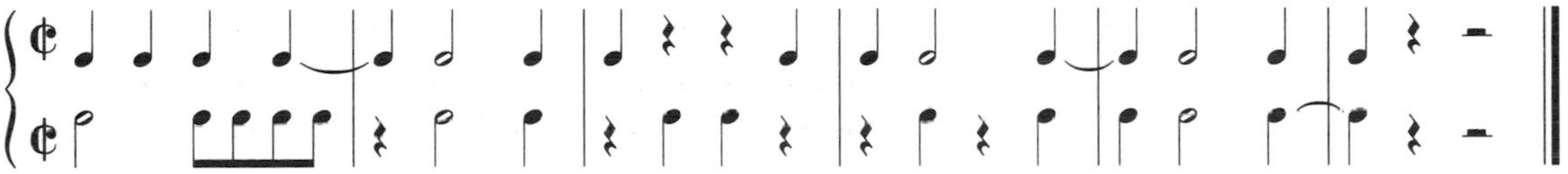

55.
56.
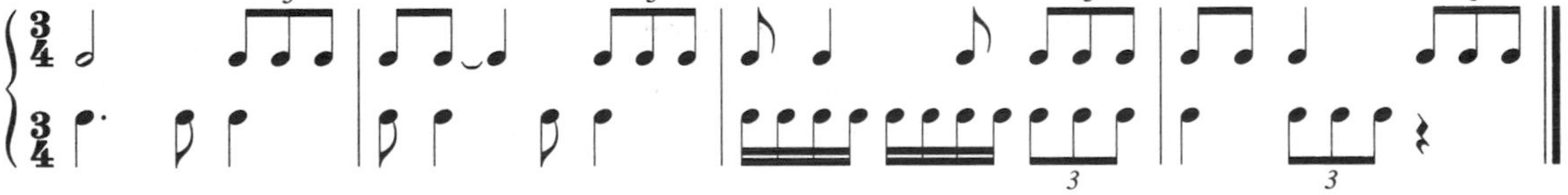

57.
58.
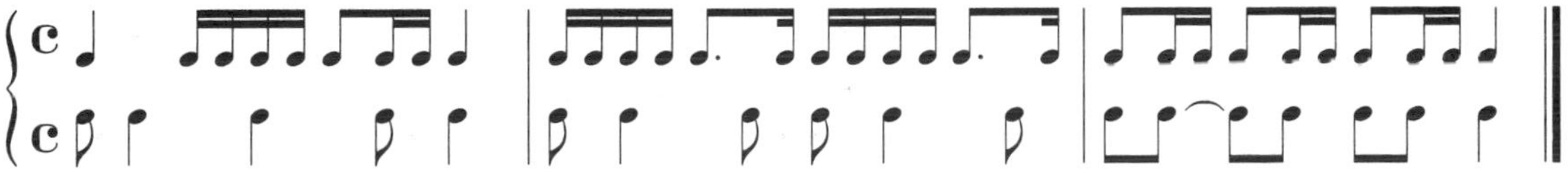

59.
60.

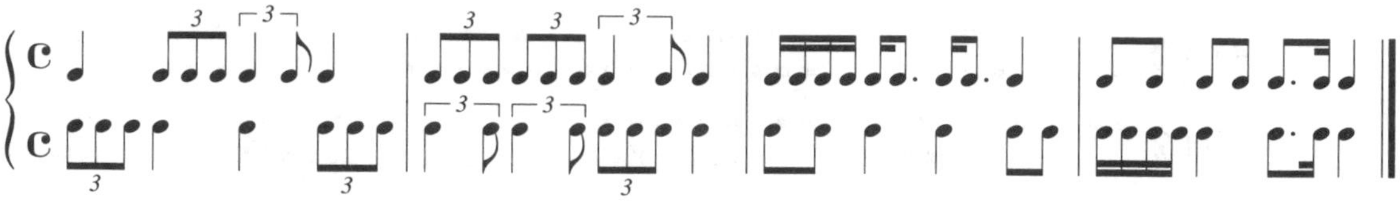

61.
62.

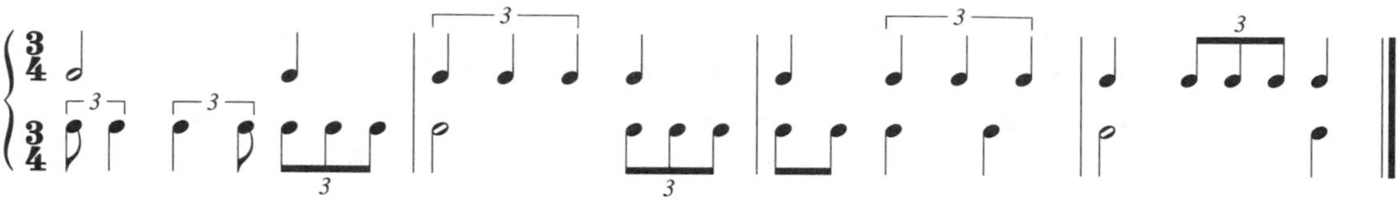

63.
64.

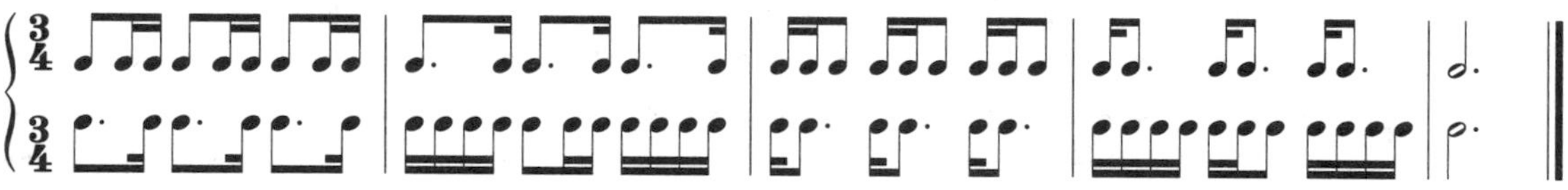

65.
66.

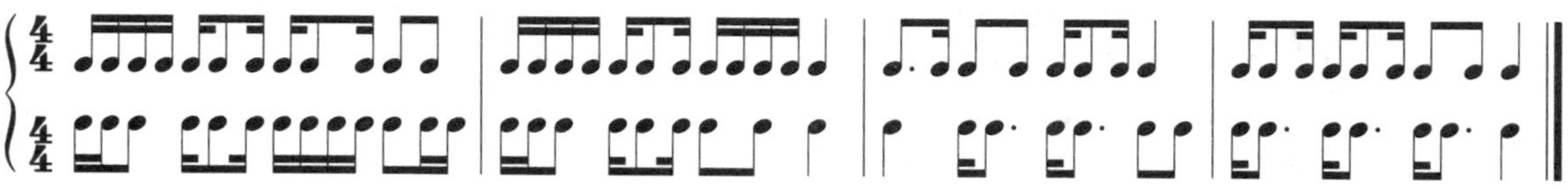

appendix **D**

Rhythms for Dictation

- Find someone who can read music notation and have that person play some of these rhythm dictation exercises for you. If no one is available to help, make your own tape recording of these exercises and play them back so that you can memorize them and practice notating them.
- Appendix C, Rhythm Studies, may also be used for dictation exercises.

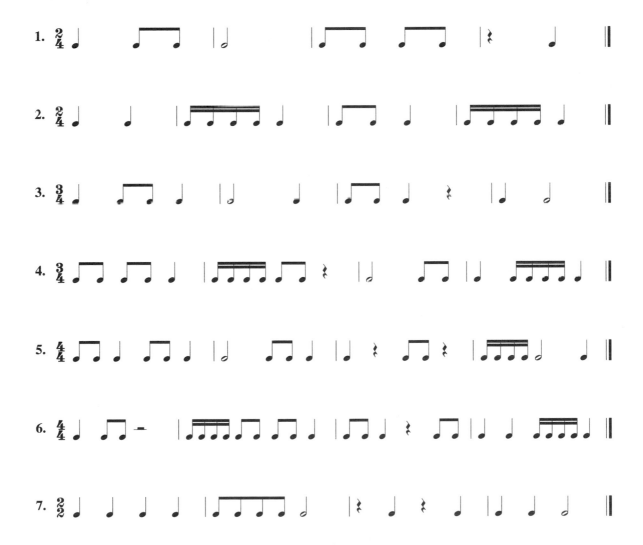

8. $\mathbf{\large \mathcal{C}}$

9. $\mathbf{\large \frac{6}{8}}$

10. $\mathbf{\large \frac{6}{8}}$

appendix **E**

Melodic Studies

- Sing these exercises at slow, moderate, and fast tempos while using a metronome to tap a steady beat.
- Before performing, sing the scale and the primary chords used in each melody; this will make hearing the pitches easier.
- Learn to play these melodies on the piano—treble-clef melodies with the right hand, and bass-clef melodies with the left hand.
- After becoming proficient at playing these melodies, add a simple right- or left-hand chordal accompaniment to your performance. See Appendix G for suggested accompaniment patterns.

appendix **F**

Melodies for Dictation

- Find someone who can read music notation and have that person play some of these melodic dictation exercises for you. If no one is available to help, make your own tape recording of these exercises and play them back so that you can memorize them and practice notating them.
- Appendix E, Melodic Studies, may also be used for dictation exercises.

9.

10.

appendix **G**

Chord Accompaniment Patterns for Piano

- These chord patterns use the primary chords tonic (I, C major), subdominant (IV, F major), and dominant seventh (V^7, G dom. 7th) in the key of C major.

- Lowering the third of the tonic and subdominant triads of these patterns changes the key to C minor (i, C minor), (iv, F minor), (V^7, G dom. 7th), the parallel minor of C major.

- Notice that the notation and the fingering for the first pattern are given for both the left hand (1a) and the right hand (1b). All patterns may be played with either the left or the right hand. If the melody is in the right hand, play the accompaniment with the left; if the melody is in the left hand, play the accompaniment with the right.

- Also notice that these patterns use root position for the I chord, second inversion for the IV_4^6 chord, and first inversion for the V_5^6 chord.

- The chord sequence used in these examples (I–IV_4^6–V_5^6–I) may be changed or expanded to fit any melody (I–V_5^6–I–IV_4^6–I, etc.). The missing fifth (D) of the V_5^6 may be substituted for the seventh (F) to replace the dominant seventh (G^7) with the dominant triad (G).

- The fingering for each chord remains the same regardless of the chord sequence or the pattern being performed.

- These patterns may be transposed to any major or minor key. Practice playing the patterns over and over in all twelve major and minor keys until you develop *muscle memory* in your hands. Muscle memory lets your fingers move quickly with an intelligence of their own.

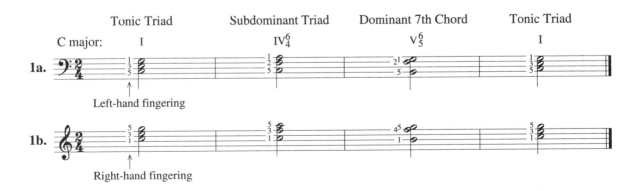

211

appendix H

Recorded Examples Not Notated within Text

9.11
a. min. 2nd b. perf. oct. c. tritone d. maj. 3rd e. perf. oct. f. maj. 6th
g. maj. 2nd h. maj. 7th i. perf. 4th j. min. 3rd k. perf. 4th l. maj. 6th
m. tritone n. maj. 2nd o. min. 6th p. maj. 7th q. min. 7th r. perf. 5th
s. min. 3rd t. maj. 3rd u. min. 2nd v. min. 6th w. perf. 5th x. min. 7th

9.18
a. min. 6th b. min. 2nd c. maj. 3rd d. tritone e. min. 7th f. perf. 5th
g. min. 2nd h. perf. oct. i. min. 7th j. tritone k. min. 3rd l. maj. 7th
m. min. 3rd n. perf. 5th o. maj. 2nd p. maj. 6th q. perf. 4th r. min. 6th
s. perf. 4th t. maj. 2nd u. perf. oct. v. maj. 7th w. maj. 3rd x. maj. 6th

Chapter 9, Assignment 8

9.20a *Melodic intervals*

1. min. 3rd
2. perf. 4th
3. maj. 2nd
4. min. 6th

5. min. 7th
6. maj. 3rd
7. tritone
8. perf. 5th

9. maj. 7th
10. min. 2nd
11. maj. 6th
12. perf. oct.

9.20b *Harmonic intervals*

1. min. 3rd
2. maj. 7th
3. perf. 4th
4. maj. 6th

5. maj. 2nd
6. maj. 3rd
7. tritone
8. perf. 5th

9. min. 2nd
10. min. 6th
11. perf. oct.
12. min. 7th

10.10
a. dis. b. con. c. con. d. con. e. dis. f. dis.
g. con. h. con. i. dis. j. dis. k. con. l. dis.

10.12
a. maj. b. maj. c. min. d. min. e. min. f. maj.
g. maj. h. maj. i. maj. j. min. k. min. l. min.

10.14
a. dim. b. aug. c. aug. d. dim. e. dim. f. aug.
g. aug. h. aug. i. dim. j. dim. k. aug. l. dim.

10.15
a. min. b. aug. c. maj. d. min. e. dim. f. aug.
g. maj. h. dim. i. aug. j. min. k. dim. l. maj.
m. aug. n. dim. o. min. p. maj. q. aug. r. maj.
s. dim. t. min. u. maj. v. dim. w. aug. x. min.

Chapter 10, Assignment 4

10.23a *Melodic intervals*

1. min. 3rd
2. perf. 4th
3. maj. 2nd
4. min. 6th

5. perf. 5th
6. maj. 6th
7. tritone
8. min. 7th

9. perf. oct.
10. min. 2nd
11. maj. 7th
12. maj. 3rd

10.23b *Harmonic intervals*

1. min. 3rd	5. min. 2nd	9. perf. 5th
2. tritone	6. min. 7th	10. maj. 7th
3. maj. 2nd	7. maj. 3rd	11. maj. 6th
4. min. 6th	8. perf. 4th	12. perf. oct.

10.23c *Triads and dominant seventh chords in root position*

1. maj.	5. dom. 7th	9. aug.
2. min.	6. dim.	10. min.
3. aug.	7. aug.	11. maj.
4. dim.	8. min.	12. dom. 7th

Chapter 10, Assignment 5

10.24

appendix *I*

Jazz-Style Guitar Chord Voicings

- The following guitar chord voicings may be used to perform examples 13.1–13.6, written below.

- These voicings may also be used for performing jazz and popular music.

- Letters and numbers above the chord frame represent the following: X, string not played or muted; R, root of chord; 3rd, 5th, 7th, 9th, or 13th of chord.

- Although these chord voicings are placed on the chord frames in the keys of C major and C minor, they are all movable to other frets and can be used to play the same chord qualities on any of the twelve tones.

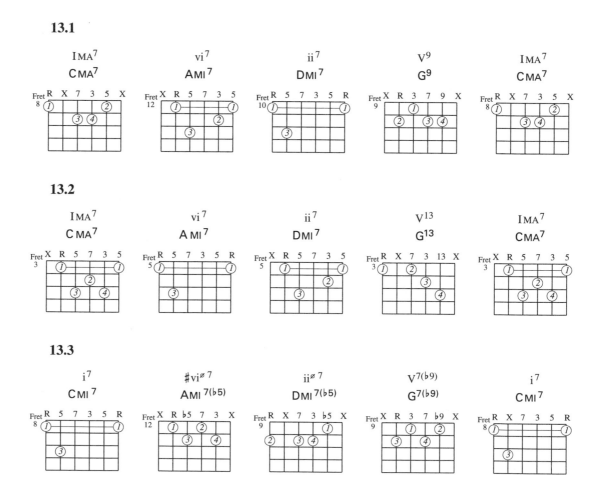

13.1

| I MA⁷ | vi⁷ | ii⁷ | V⁹ | I MA⁷ |
| CMA⁷ | AMI⁷ | DMI⁷ | G⁹ | CMA⁷ |

13.2

| I MA⁷ | vi⁷ | ii⁷ | V¹³ | I MA⁷ |
| CMA⁷ | AMI⁷ | DMI⁷ | G¹³ | CMA⁷ |

13.3

| i⁷ | #vi∅⁷ | ii∅⁷ | V⁷⁽♭⁹⁾ | i⁷ |
| CMI⁷ | AMI⁷⁽♭⁵⁾ | DMI⁷⁽♭⁵⁾ | G⁷⁽♭⁹⁾ | CMI⁷ |

13.4

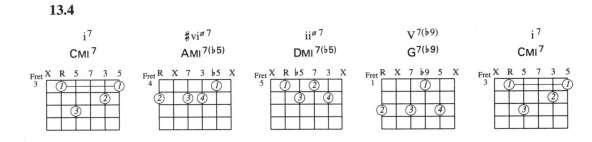

13.5 *C major blues*

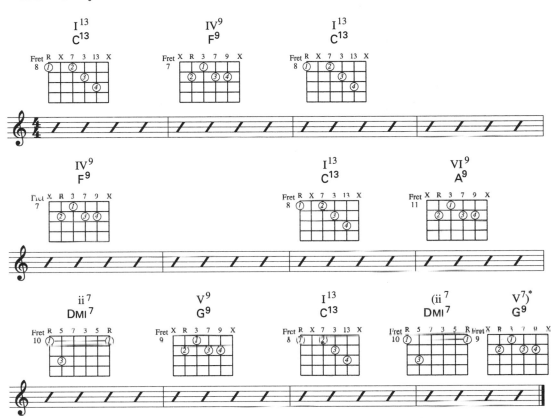

* These chords are played only when repeating this blues progression.

13.6   *C minor blues*

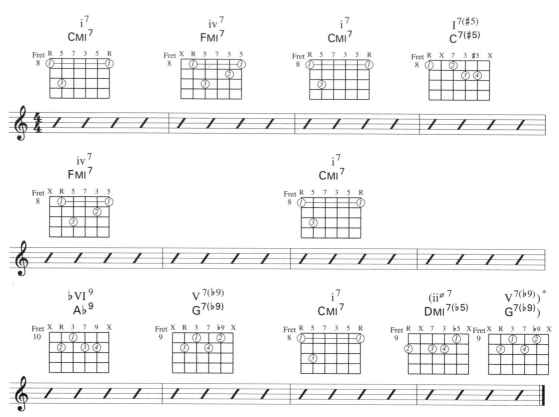

* These chords are played only when repeating this blues progression.

Rhythms Used for Comping Jazz Harmonies

- When a keyboardist or a guitarist creates a harmonized accompaniment from chord symbols, he or she improvises chord voicings and rhythms to fit the style of the piece being accompanied. This technique is called **comping.**

- Below are a few rhythms that may be used in various combinations to comp chords in a jazz "swing" style. Some chord voicings for piano are suggested in Chapter 13, and some guitar voicings are given in Appendix I.

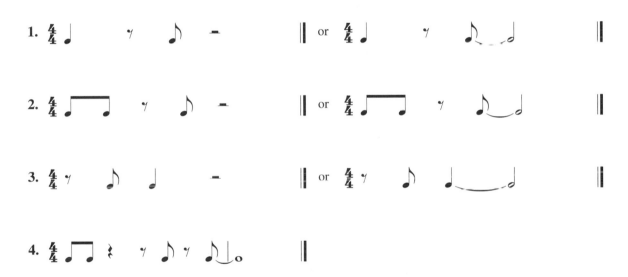

Index

A

Accent, 8
Accidentals, 13, 64
   double flat (♭♭), 76
   double sharp (✖), 76
   flat (♭), 13
   natural (♮), 13
   sharp (♯), 13
Adagio, 5, 21
Aeolian mode, 51
Alla breve (¢), 142
Allegro, 5, 21
Alto clef, 35
Anacrusis, 27
Arpeggios, 87
Artificial scales, 56
Atonal music, 58
Augmented interval, 99
Augmented scale, 57
Augmented triad, 118
Authentic cadence, 156

B

Bar line, 20
Bass clef, 35
Beat, 3, 6
Black keys, 13
Blues scales, 56
Borrowed rhythm patterns, 147
Broken chords, 87

C

Cadence, 3, 156
   authentic, 156
   plagal, 156

C-clef, 35
Chord(s), 3, 117
   primary, 87, 135
   secondary, 156
   seventh, 128
      inversions of, 133
   triads, 3, 118
      inversions of, 131
Chord progression, 135
   modulation, 164
Chord voicings, 169
Chorus, 186
Chromaticism, 57
Chromatic scale, 56
Church modes, 51
Circle of fifths, 74
Classifications of triads, 118
Clef sign, 34
   alto clef, 35
   C-clef, 35
   F-clef (bass), 35
   G-clef (treble), 34
   tenor clef, 35
   viola clef, 35
Common time (𝐜), 21
Comping, 219
Compound duple meter, 9, 144, 145
Compound intervals, 101
Compound meters, 20, 144, 145
   duple, 144, 145
   quadruple, 145
   triple, 145
Compound notes, 20, 27
Compound quadruple meter, 145
Compound triple meter, 9, 145
Consonant harmonic intervals, 110

Consonant triads, 121
Contrast, 45
Crescendo, 5, 28
Cut time (₵), 142

D

D.C. al Fine, 78
Decrescendo, 5, 28
Diatonic scale, 50
Diminished cycle, 176
Diminished interval, 99
Diminished scale, 57
Diminished triad, 118
Diminuendo, 28
Dissonant harmonic intervals, 110
Dissonant triads, 121
Dolce, 5
Dominant, 87, 130, 135
Dominant seventh chord, 3, 5, 130
Dorian mode, 51
Dot, 27
Dotted half note, 27
Dotted quarter note, 27
Double bar line, 20
Double flat (♭♭), 76
Double sharp (✗), 76
Duple meter, 8
Duplet, 147
Dynamic markings, 5, 28
    crescendo, 5, 28
    decrescendo, 5, 28
    diminuendo, 28
    f, 5, 28
    ff, 28
    mf, 5, 28
    mp, 5, 28
    p, 5, 28
    pp, 28
Dynamics, 5, 28

E

Early One Morning, 78
Eighth note, 22
Eighth rest, 25
Eleventh, 101
Enharmonic pitches, 13
Equal temperament, 52
Exact repetition, 45

F

f, 5, 28
F-clef, 35
Fermata, 27
ff, 28
Final double bar line, 20
First inversion, 131, 133

Fixed-*do* system, 84
Flat (♭), 13
Form, 1, 185–86
    three-part, 185
    three-part song, 186
    through-composed, 185
    two-part, 185
    two-part song, 186
Forte (*f*), 5, 28
Fortissimo (*ff*), 28

G

G-clef, 34
Grand staff, 35
Great staff, 35
Greensleeves, 79
Gypsy scale, 55

H

Half note, 22
Half rest, 25
Half step, 12, 50
Harmonic interval, 98
Harmonic minor scale, 54, 75
Harmonic tones, 135
Harmonization, 135, 162, 176
Harmony, 3
    quartal, 117
    tertian, 117
Hold, 27
Hungarian scale, 55
Hybrid scales, 56

I

Improvisation, 10, 17
Incomplete measure, 27
Interval, 12, 98–103, 106
    augmented, 99
    compound, 101
    diminished, 99
    harmonic, 98
    inverted, 103
    major, 99
    melodic, 98
    minor, 99
    perfect, 99
    simple, 101
Interval quality, 99
Interval size, 99
Inversions, 103, 131, 133
    of intervals, 103
    of seventh chords, 133
    of triads, 131
Inverted diminished scale, 58
Ionian mode, 51
Irregular rhythm patterns, 148

J

Joshua Fought the Battle of Jericho, 78
Just intonation, 52
Just Sing It! 2, 89, 91, 92, 162, 174

K

Key, 58
Keyboard, 6, 13
    black keys, 13
    white keys, 13
Keynote, 58
Key signature, 63, 64, 66, 71

L

Leading tone, 130
Ledger lines, 35
Letter sight-singing method, 84
Locrian mode, 51
Lydian mode, 51
Lyrics, 1, 180

M

Major interval, 99
Major key signatures, 66, 71
Major/minor tonal system, 52
Major pentatonic scale, 55
Major scale, 53
Major triad, 118
Measure, 20
Mediant, 130
Melodic dictation, 42
Melodic interval, 98
Melodic minor scale, 54, 75
Melody, 3
Meter, 8
    compound, 144, 145
    mixed, 140
    multimetric, 140
    simple, 20, 144, 145
Meter signature, 20
Metronome, 6
Mezzo (*m*), 5, 28
    mezzo forte (*mf*), 5, 28
    mezzo piano (*mp*), 5, 28
mf, 5, 28
Minor interval, 99
Minor key signatures, 66, 71
Minor pentatonic scale, 55
Minor scales, 53, 75
    harmonic, 54, 75
    melodic, 54, 75
    natural, 53, 75
Minor third–half-step scale, 57
Minor triad, 118
Mixed meter, 140
Mixolydian mode, 51

M.M., 6
Modality, 58
Modal scales, 51
    aeolian, 51
    dorian, 51
    ionian, 51
    locrian, 51
    lydian, 51
    mixolydian, 51
    phrygian, 51
Moderato, 5, 21
Modes, 51
Modulation, 164
Motive, 45
Movable-*do* system, 84
mp, 5, 28
Multimetric, 140
Music, 6
Musical expression, 5

N

Natural (♮), 13
Natural minor scale, 53, 75
Ninth, 101
Nonchord tones, 136
Nonharmonic tones, 136
Nontuplet, 148
Notation, 19, 25, 36
Notes, 19
Note values, 19
Numeral sight-singing method, 84

O

Octatonic scale, 57
Octave, 13

P

p, 5, 28
Parallel major and minor scales, 53, 66–68
Passionato, 5
Pedal tone, 177
Pentatonic scales, 55
    major, 55
    minor, 55
Perfect interval, 99
Period, 3
Phrase, 3
Phrasing, 5
Phrygian mode, 51
Pianissimo (*pp*), 28
Piano (*p*), 5, 28
Pickup, 27
Pitch, 2
Pitch notation, 34
Pitch range, 12
Plagal cadence, 156

Planing, 177
Polychord symbol, 170
pp, 28
Primary chords, 87, 135
    dominant, 87, 135
    subdominant, 87, 135
    tonic, 87, 135

Q
Quadruple meter, 8
Quadruplet, 148
Quality
    interval, 99
    triad, 118
Quartal harmony, 117
Quarter note, 21
Quarter rest, 25
Quintuplet, 148

R
Refrain, 186
Register, 12
Relative major and minor scales, 66–68
Repeat sign, 37, 38, 92
Repetition, 45
    exact, 45
    sequential, 45
    varied, 45
Rest, 25
Rest notation, 25
Rest values, 25
Rhythm, 3
Rhythm dictation, 29
Rhythm notation, 19
Rhythm syllables, 23
Rock-A My Soul, 187
Roman numeral symbols, 124
Root, 118, 133
Root position, 131, 133

S
Scale, 3, 50, 53, 75
    harmonic minor, 54, 75
    major, 53
    melodic minor, 54, 75
    natural minor, 53, 75
Scarborough Fair, 185
Secondary chords, 156
Secondary dominant seventh, 165
Second inversion, 131, 133
Semitone, 50
Septuplet, 148
Sequence, 45
Sequential repetition, 45
Seventh chords, 128, 133
    inversions of, 133

Sextuplet, 147
Sharp (♯), 13
Sight singing, 84
    letter sight-singing method, 84
    numeral sight-singing method, 84
    solfeggio systems, 84
        fixed-*do,* 84
        movable-*do,* 84
Simple duple meter, 9, 20, 144, 145
Simple intervals, 101
Simple meters, 20, 144, 145
    alla breve (¢), 142
    cut time (¢), 142
    duple, 9, 20, 144, 145
    quadruple, 10, 20, 145
    triple, 9, 20, 145
Simple notes, 20
Simple quadruple meter, 10, 20, 145
Simple triple meter, 9, 20, 145
Sixteenth note, 22
Size (interval), 99
Solfeggio systems, 84
Song, 179
Songs
    Early One Morning, 78
    Greensleeves, 79
    Joshua Fought the Battle of Jericho, 78
    Just Sing It! 2, 89, 91, 92, 162, 174
    Rock-A My Soul, 187
    Scarborough Fair, 185
    Water Come to Me Eye, 186
Staff, 34
Stanza, 180
Stave, 34
Strophic song, 185
Subdominant, 87, 130, 135
Submediant, 130
Subtonic, 130
Supertonic, 130
Symmetrical scales, 56
Syncopated rhythm, 149
Synthetic scales, 56

T
Tempi, 5
Tempo, 3
Tempos, 5
Tenor clef, 35
Tenth, 101
Tertian harmony, 117
Third inversion, 133
Thirteenth, 101
Three-part form, 185
Three-part song form, 186
Through-composed form, 185
Tie, 26
Time, 3

Time signature, 20
Tonal center, 58
Tonality, 58
Tonic, 58, 87, 130, 135
Touch, 5
Transposition, 59
Treble clef, 34
Triad(s), 3, 118
    augmented, 118
    classifications of, 118
    consonant, 121
    diminished, 118
    dissonant, 121
    letter name of, 118
    major, 4, 118
    minor, 118
    quality of, 118
    root of, 118, 131
Triad inversions, 131
Triple meter, 8
Triplet, 147
Tritone, 106
Tritone substitution, 176

Twelfth, 101
Twelve basic interval sounds, 106, 108
Twelve-tone pitch system, 13
Two-part form, 185
Two-part song form, 186

U
Unaccented beats, 8

V
Varied repetition, 45
Verse, 180
Viola clef, 35

W
Water Come to Me Eye, 186
White keys, 13
Whole note, 19
Whole rest, 25
Whole step, 13, 50
Whole tone, 50
Whole-tone scale, 57